Praise for *The P*

"[Pollack] tells us, with a clarity unu
works."                                    —F.

"*The Pun Also Rises* is a brief but compelling exegesis on what puns are
and why they matter."                                    —*Los Angeles Times*

"The best books on language are the ones that encourage us to reexamine
what we think we know, and *The Pun Also Rises,* a new book on 'the lowest form of wit,' does exactly that."                                    —*The Boston Globe*

"O. Henry Pun-Off World Champion John Pollack's new book *The Pun
Also Rises* lives up to its ambitious subtitle."                                    --*The Huffington Post*

"It's fascinating and funny."                                    —*Brave New Words*

"*The Pun Also Rises* is refreshingly witty, intelligent, and informative."
                                    – *Rundpinne*

"Whether you are a practicing punster, interested in language, or just
hungry to learn something on the beach this summer as you lie on the
sand-which-is there . . . Pollack's book is fun and informative."
                                    —*Detroit Free Press*

"[A]n engrossing history of the pun."                                    —*The Globe and Mail* (Toronto)

"If you're at all interested in language, and how it has shaped humanity,
read this book. You won't be disappointed."                                    —*Reading Through Life*

"*The Pun Also Rises* is one of those simple pleasures of the book world: a
thoroughly entertaining book that's also academic, so you can feel smart
and learn new jokes at the same time."                                    —*The Huntsville Item*

"It's a fascinating history, and the book is an awful lot of fun."
                                    —Joe Donahue, WAMC

"An entertaining and illuminating exploration of how wordplay evolved
to be much more than a cheap linguistic thrill or the product of bottom-
feeder copywriters."                                    —Maria Popova, *Brain Pickings*

"A fun, cogent argument in favor of a dubious, often-damned art."
                                    —*Kirkus Reviews*

"In *The Pun Also Rises*, John Pollack stirs the brain and tickles the funny
bone with rewording insights into why the pun is dramatically rising in
our culture. We discover that the much maligned pun is, in truth, much

aligned language in which two or more meanings occupy the same verbal space at the same time. With dazzling whiz and witdom, the author illuminates how the pun has made us who we are today."

—Richard Lederer, International Punster of the Year
and author of *Get Thee to a Punnery*

"With his compelling narrative style, Pollack unearths hard evidence to bolster his case for the legitimacy of the noble pun as much more than a literary stepchild or linguistic anomaly. As a practitioner of the art and artifice of wordplay himself, John naturally dedicates a bit of spice to peppering and assaulting us with a few subtle zingers of his zone."

—Gary Hallock, producer of the
O. Henry Pun-Off World Championships

"Punderful!"     —Ben Schott, author of *Schott's Original Miscellany*

© DAVE TURNLEY

**John Pollack,** who won the 1995 O. Henry Pun-Off World Championships, was a presidential speechwriter for Bill Clinton. Earlier, he worked as a foreign correspondent in Spain, as a field assistant in Antarctica, and as a strolling violinist on Mackinac Island. He is the author of *Cork Boat: A True Story of the Unlikeliest Boat Ever Built.* He lives in New York City.

# The Pun Also Rises

HOW THE HUMBLE PUN
REVOLUTIONIZED LANGUAGE,
CHANGED HISTORY,
AND MADE WORDPLAY
MORE THAN SOME ANTICS

JOHN POLLACK

GOTHAM BOOKS

GOTHAM BOOKS
Published by Penguin Group (USA) Inc.
375 Hudson Street, New York, New York 10014, U.S.A.
Penguin Group (Canada), 90 Eglinton Avenue East, Suite 700, Toronto, Ontario M4P 2Y3,
Canada (a division of Pearson Penguin Canada Inc.) • Penguin Books Ltd, 80 Strand, London
WC2R 0RL, England • Penguin Ireland, 25 St Stephen's Green, Dublin 2, Ireland (a division
of Penguin Books Ltd) • Penguin Group (Australia), 250 Camberwell Road, Camberwell,
Victoria 3124, Australia (a division of Pearson Australia Group Pty Ltd) • Penguin Books
India Pvt Ltd, 11 Community Centre, Panchsheel Park, New Delhi–110 017, India • Penguin
Group (NZ), 67 Apollo Drive, Rosedale, Auckland 0632, New Zealand (a division of Pearson
New Zealand Ltd) • Penguin Books (South Africa) (Pty) Ltd, 24 Sturdee Avenue, Rosebank,
Johannesburg 2196, South Africa

Penguin Books Ltd, Registered Offices: 80 Strand, London WC2R 0RL, England

Published by Gotham Books, a member of Penguin Group (USA) Inc.

Previously published as a Gotham Books hardcover edition

First trade paperback printing, February 2012

10  9  8  7  6  5  4

Gotham Books and the skyscraper logo are trademarks of Penguin Group (USA) Inc.

Copyright © 2011 by John Pollack

All rights reserved. No part of this book may be reproduced, scanned, or distributed in any
printed or electronic form without permission. Please do not participate in or encourage
piracy of copyrighted materials in violation of the author's rights. Purchase only authorized
editions.

The Library of Congress has Cataloged the hardcover edition of this book as follows:

Pollack, John.
The pun also rises : how the humble pun revolutionized language, changed history, and
made wordplay more than some antics / John Pollack.
    p. cm.
  Includes bibliographical references.
  ISBN 978-1-592-40623-4 (hardcover)  978-1-592-40675-3 (paperback)
  1.  Puns and punning.    2.  English language—Humor  I. Title.
  PN6231.W64P65 2011
  808.7—dc22          2011004318

Printed in the United States of America

*Set in Granjon*    •    *Designed by Catherine Leonardo*

The scanning, uploading, and distribution of this book via the Internet or via any other
means without the permission of the publisher is illegal and punishable by law. Please purchase only authorized electronic editions, and do not participate in or encourage electronic
piracy of copyrighted materials. Your support of the author's rights is appreciated.

While the author has made every effort to provide accurate telephone numbers and Internet
addresses at the time of publication, neither the publisher nor the author assumes any responsibility for errors, or for changes that occur after publication. Further, the publisher does not
have any control over and does not assume any responsibility for author or third-party Web
sites or their content.

*To the 10th Street Gang*

# CONTENTS

Language, be it remembered, is not an abstract construction of the learned, or of dictionary-makers, but is something arising out of the work, needs, ties, joys, affections, tastes of long generations of humanity, and has its bases broad and low, close to the ground. Its final decisions are made by the masses, people nearest the concrete, having most to do with actual land and sea. It permeates us all, the past as well as the present, and is the grandest triumph of the human intellect.

--Walt Whitman

# Bears Go Barefoot

LIGHTNING FLASHED, THE PLANE BUCKED, AND ANOTHER GASP swept the cabin. I cinched my seat belt even tighter and stole another glance into the inky abyss, where I could just make out the red light on the jet's wingtip, flapping like a bird.

The plane shuddered again, and I thought of the SS *Edmund Fitzgerald*, a giant ore freighter that had snapped in two during a fierce gale when I was a boy, plunging into the icy depths of Lake Superior. The wreck had been big news in my home state of Michigan. The ship, longer than a football field, had sunk so fast that the captain didn't even have time to radio an SOS. All hands were lost.

Tonight, at odds with the gods in this riveted aluminum tube some thirty thousand feet above the Ozarks, I tried to push that ship from my mind, but couldn't. At least, not until what felt like a giant fist suddenly smashed the plane from above, as if an angry Zeus were trying to crush a beer can. In an instant, some two hundred yellow oxygen masks dropped from the ceiling and the plane nosed into a sudden, steep descent.

The announcement that followed was familiar but startling in its reality: "Please place the mask over your nose and mouth and breathe normally."

For the next several minutes I breathed cold, pure oxygen and felt, in the pit of my stomach, the altitude falling away. My decision to board this flight to Austin, Texas, had been somewhat impulsive—a journey of choice to compete in an absurd contest: the eighteenth annual world pun championships. I had secured a spot in the tournament only ten days earlier, after punning with the organizer over the phone. He'd seemed reluctant to have me fly down at first, but he needed one last competitor to fill an early bracket. Why not a sacrificial lamb from Michigan?

Like a boxer sparring before a big fight, I'd spent the ensuing week punning with my dad—like me, a proud punster—training myself to come up with successive puns in five seconds or less. According to the rules, I'd be paired with an opponent and given a topic. Alternating, each of us would have five seconds to respond with a pun on that topic, back and forth, until someone missed. It would be single elimination. If I came up blank just once, or if the judge ruled that a pun I'd made was not actually a pun, I'd be out.

Apart from internalizing the five-second deadline, there wasn't much I could do to prepare that would add or detract from my punning abilities. I'd been playing with words since I learned to talk. In fact, my first complete sentence in life had been a pun. As my mom tells the story, I was two and a half years old and still struggling to string a sentence together—a skill some kids pick up earlier. "I guess he's just a little slow," she thought.

Then one morning I toddled into the kitchen. "Johnny," she said. "Go get your shoes. I don't want you walking barefoot."

I looked up at her, put my hand over my mouth and giggled impishly.

"Bears go barefoot!" I said.

And I've been punning ever since.

As the plane dropped, I had to concede that if my number really was up, at least I would go down en route to the world championships. Far better a plane crash in the sticks than a car accident on my daily commute into the Detroit suburbs, where I worked as a project manager at The Henry Ford museum.

My mortal concerns were, fortunately, premature. Somewhere below ten thousand feet, the plane leveled off. The captain, coming on the intercom for the first time, apologized for the turbulence, assured us everything was under control and told us that we could remove our masks. Apart from all those masks dangling from the ceiling, the rest of the flight seemed almost normal.

Two days later, I stood on a stage in an Austin park outside the O. Henry Museum, looking out over a crowd I estimated at five hundred people and trying to calm myself as the emcee—a tall Texan in a straw hat—introduced me and my opponent. I was already outmatched; my adversary was a bespectacled, forty-something man named George McClughan who, as the judge pointed out, just happened to be a former champion. Talk about a bad draw.

After reviewing the rules, the judge asked McClughan to

reach into a galvanized bucket and pull out a slip of paper, which featured one of the hundred or so topics on a list that my thirty-one fellow competitors and I had been given just minutes earlier. There had been too many to actually study, but enough to make my mouth go dry with fear. What if I froze, and couldn't come up with a single pun?

The judge read McClughan's slip aloud: "Air Vehicles."

"George, why don't you go ahead and start," the judge said.

"Oh, all right," my opponent said. He looked so relaxed just standing there at the microphone, his shirt untucked, smiling at the crowd. And why not? He was a seasoned champion, and I was just some no-name walk-on from Michigan.

"If a helicopter had babies," McClughan asked, "would it be a baby Huey?" It took me a moment to get it—a clever reference to both the cartoon duck and the workhorse chopper of Vietnam. He was going to flatten me.

My mind flashed to all the aircraft hanging from the rafters back at The Henry Ford museum. "I hope I come up with the Wright Flying Machine," I said.

"Wait, wait . . ." It was the judge, holding up his hand. "It's gotta be a puh-un." In his Texas drawl, pun was almost a two-syllable word.

"The Wright Brothers," I said. "W-R-I-G-H-T—I hope I pick the Wright Flying Machine."

A sudden cheer swept the audience. The brawl was on.

"That was so plane to see," McClughan said, grinning.

I struggled to come up with a response, but saved myself at the last second with a crude pun on Fokker, the defunct Dutch aircraft maker.

McClughan didn't flinch. "I guess if I'm going to B-52 next week I'm never going to C-47 again," he said.

"Well . . . ," I said, scanning the audience, "I'm looking for a Liberator out there."

McClughan toyed with me. "This guy's pretty good," he said. "I was hoping he'd B-1 bomber."

I was finding my rhythm. "You don't think I'd take to flight, do you?"

"I don't know," he answered casually. "You're just up here winging it."

"U-2?"

In its economy and perfect congruence of sound and meaning, a pun couldn't get any purer. I could pun for an entire lifetime and never make a better one, ever. It was a knockout punch, and the crowd roared. But that rangy Texan refused to fall.

"A bear made pies for its babies," he replied. "One Piper Cub."

And so it went, pun after pun, as we pummeled each other—and the English language—without mercy. From aircraft parts to the space program to the Battle of Britain, McClughan always had a good riposte ready. He was, in a word, unflappable.

"My girlfriend Mimi came over last night, and we had sex," he bragged. "She was a real screaming Mimi." An obscure reference, but valid. The Screaming Mimi was a type of German rocket artillery from World War II.

From the storm clouds of my subconscious, a Japanese warplane zoomed down to counterattack. "I heard that was a Zero."

The crowd was still cheering when the bell rang. Our seven-minute round was over. Exhausted, I stood there for a moment, heart pounding, mouth dry, my brain seizing up like an overheated engine that's run out of oil. A little dazed at my survival, I turned to walk off the stage.

"John! John! John!" It was the judge. "Don't go anywhere. You've got the Wright Patter, son."

I returned to my microphone. In the case of a tie, the judge explained, the audience got to decide who advanced to the next round. I looked out at the audience. Whatever happened, I could go home proud; at least I hadn't crashed and burned.

The vote wasn't unanimous, but when asked to cheer for the "punster of note," the crowd chose me. I don't know who was more stunned, me or McClughan. A gentleman to the last, though, he shook my hand warmly. Almost in a stupor, I made my way off the stage in search of the concession stand. Before facing my next opponent, I needed a round I could really en-joy—a cold beer.

For the next hour or so, I watched others compete and mar-veled at their brilliant wordplay. One contestant, a pudgy fel-low with a bristly mustache and nasal voice, was particularly talented. By day, he worked as a paramedic. Onstage, he was a butcher, dismembering his opponent pun by pun. Word had it he was so competitive that he actually spent the off-season (in this case, all year) studying videos of championships past— gleaning technique, building up a repertoire, honing his skills. And year by year, he'd been climbing through the ranks. Twelve months earlier, he'd finished third.

Knowing it would be tough to advance, I just tried to savor my first-round victory and enjoy the show. All too soon, though, the announcer called my name and that of my next opponent. Downing the last of my beer, I hurried up to the stage, only to discover that my adversary was the paramedic punster himself.

The judge announced the topic: "Historical facts about the state of Michigan."

I gulped.

"Just kidding," the judge said, laughing. "The subject is football."

"Nice try," the paramedic said, smirking.

And off we went, trading bad puns on every conceivable aspect of the game. It quickly became apparent that the paramedic had a one-track mind. "I can't wait until this is over," he said in an early exchange, "so I can find a woman with a tight end."

A few puns later, he returned to sex again. "Let me get back to the subject of that would-be lady friend. One of the things she always liked about me was the Longhorn."

Even though we were just a mile or so from the Texas campus, a chorus of boos rippled through the crowd. Apparently, I wasn't the only one who was starting to understand just why his would-be girlfriend was hypothetical.

"I think my energy is running low, and his energy is running low," I said, trying to steer the exchange in a better direction. "We need to call up the Chargers."

But apparently he didn't need energy—he needed to get laid. "Getting back to that hypothetical girlfriend," he said, "I'd like to Raider treasures."

Mercifully, the bell rang. Our seven minutes were up, and I had survived. Still, by any measure, the paramedic had gotten off more good puns and would probably win the vote.

To my surprise, the judge asked the audience if we should just keep going on football until one of us lost. The crowd roared its approval.

The puns I offered in the next few exchanges were barely

puns, interspersed with a lot of "uhs" and "ums" as I stalled for time. Despite my difficulties, I refused to surrender. Without mercy, he drove me backward pun by pun. "One of the best things about dating," he said, "is that there's a lot of Ramming involved."

The crowd booed. I was grateful for the extra moment's delay because I couldn't think of another pun to save my life. Defeat lay just five seconds away. Four seconds. Three. I guess I just wasn't cut out to be world champion. Two. Wait . . . champion . . . breakfast of champions . . . breakfast!

"Maybe we should all have breakfast," I said quickly, "and eat some Gippers and eggs."

"The Sooner the better," he answered, referring to the University of Oklahoma mascot.

"OK," I said.

On and on we went, riffing on bowl games, Big Ten teams, famous stadiums. It didn't take long for the paramedic to return to a hypothetical girlfriend—this one with a Southeast infection.

The judge had heard enough. "You want both of 'em?" he asked the audience.

They cheered, probably just to get rid of us.

In the next round, the topic was male names, and my opponent—a woman named Dale—seemed to know a lot of them. Quickly, we raced through fifty or sixty names, until none of the easy ones were left. In a moment of inspiration, I found a zinger: "In punning," I explained, "one always has to look through the crevasses of the English language and Hannibalize things."

The duel went on. Challenging me with a Cain, she proved herself Abel. Then, suddenly, she came up empty. Somehow I had managed to advance, yet again.

For the semifinals, there were five of us up onstage, including the paramedic. The topic was "countries of the world." And around the world we raced, almost faster than I could spin a globe. Countries toppled by the dozen, like proverbial Cold War dominoes.

"What a Laos-y topic," said one.

"Where do fish go on vacation?" asked another. "Finland."

"My mother used to cook chicken-fried steak in a big skillet," a former champion reminisced, in a shaggy dog setup. "Boy, I loved that Panama's."

Suddenly, like the British at Dunkirk, I found myself out of land, my back to the sea. Searching for some country—any country that hadn't already been mentioned, my mind flashed to a summer in college I'd spent doing geological fieldwork with my dad in East Africa. Through the shimmering heat of the dusty savannah, a spear of hope pierced my imagination.

"In Africa it's really hot, and explorers wore those pith helmets and shorts," I said. "That was so they could Tanzanias."

And the paramedic? He was, to no one's surprise, somewhere in the brothels of Eastern Europe. "A prostitute's favorite land?" he asked. "Poland."

The first to fall was the skillet man, whose final attempt was panned by the judge.

One of the remaining contenders remarked that "there's Norway we can keep on going like this." She had that right. I felt like my brain had been filled with sand, my mouth stuffed with steel wool. I suggested that the timekeeper show a little extra "Latviatude."

"Take some Prozac," the judge chided me.

I tried to smile. But all I could taste was a bitter paste of ego, fear, and the determination to survive. I struggled to concentrate. Had someone used Uruguay? Or was that Paraguay? Did Antarctica count as a country?

And then, in quick succession, a pair of opponents went down. There were only two of us left now—the paramedic and me.

The judge paused to announce that, for the final round, there would be a new topic.

I exhaled, and looked up into the sky, immensely relieved. I was out of countries; just about any new topic would seem like the Promised Land.

And then I heard it—external body parts.

External body parts? I was up against the paramedic on external body parts?!

The judge didn't waste any time. "You start, John."

"Well, I guess I'm a nose ahead on this one," I said.

But only briefly, as my opponent proceeded to riff off external body parts that I didn't even know had one meaning, let alone two.

I managed to counter each one in turn, but barely. Like a penguin trying not to slip off a disintegrating iceberg, I scrabbled toward higher ground.

"Eyelash you so badly now, why would I continue?" I asked.

"To avoid getting the finger?" he answered.

The judge laughed, the crowd whooped.

"He had me by a whisker on that one," I answered. Were there even any parts left?

Perhaps sensing his moment, he went in for the kill.

"John's been a real good competitor for his first time out," he said. "I've enjoyed having him as an archrival."

Again, the crowd cheered. But I refused to "knuckle under."

He battled back, insisting he was "still ahead."

I tugged on my ear, accusing him of a "lobe blow."

So low, he replied, that it sank to the "depths of his sole."

And then I drew a blank. A complete and total blank. To buy time, I began to speak. "Well . . . the answer to that one is that I am going to bend . . . I'm going to bend over and . . ."

A murmur of apprehension swept the crowd. "I'm going to bend over and . . ."

After hundreds of puns, I had absolutely nothing left. I didn't even know why I was saying I would bend over, except that every external body part in existence was lying on the slaughterhouse floor, already used.

The paramedic, who had punned his way through every round with his hands clasped firmly behind his back, hitched his thumbs in his pockets to wait, a thin smile of expectation on his face. Like a fish flopping on deck, I gasped for life.

"I . . . can't . . . quite . . . figure . . . out . . . the . . . answer . . . to . . . the . . ."

As if in slow motion, I saw the timekeeper glance at the judge and begin lifting his hand to strike the bell. At the very same moment a trickle of sweat rolled down my forehead and into my eye. And in that exact, stinging nanosecond I thought of a pun.

"I don't want to have to brow out!" I blurted.

Still alive.

And the verbal fistfight continued.

Talking as if he were stoned, the paramedic held an imaginary joint to his lips and took a hit. "I gotta get out of here," he said. "I don't want anyone to find mustache."

Flummoxed, my brain stalled again. And then, bursting from the cloud of my subconscious, another pun. "I'm going to chinnel my energy into coming up with a new pun," I said.

Unperturbed, the paramedic coolly launched into a shaggy dog story about mosquitoes in his Erie Canal. The judge rejected it. "Ear's been used. Canal's internal."

Calmly, the paramedic offered another. "Maybe I should try for a low blow," he said.

"Lobe's been used," the judge warned. "Last chance . . ."

"Well, it's a chin if you can't come up with . . ."

The judge caught the repeat before I did. "We have a winner!" he exclaimed. "From Ann Arbor, Michigan . . . John Pollack!"

Moments later, he handed me the champion's trophy—a classical column topped by the miniature, gilded rear end of a horse. I reveled in the moment, lifting the trophy above my head. What had begun as a lark had somehow become a personal epic, a test not just of wordplay, but of will itself.

I was under no illusions; I was not necessarily the best punster in Texas, let alone the world. But on this day, my wits and determination and a healthy dollop of good luck had made me champion. I had punned in five languages to win—English, French, Spanish, Yiddish, and Catalan—and I wasn't going to look a gift horse in the . . . well, the quarter-horse trophy in my hand didn't even have a mouth. So I just grinned for the both of us, savoring the thrill of unexpected victory.

CRITICS AND CURMUDGEONS OFTEN DERIDE THE PUN AS THE lowest form of humor. Others would counter that if that's true, it would make punning the foundation of all humor. A close study of history reveals, however, that the reflexive association between puns and humor is a relatively recent development. In ancient Babylonia and Greece, to wit, punning often had religious implications and could even lead to armed conflict.

In any case, punsters throughout history have served as some of the most adventurous scouts on the frontiers of language.

From the ancient Sanskrit grammarian Pāṇini (who deconstructed sandwiched meanings in the fourth century BC) to playwrights and philosophers such as Sophocles, Shakespeare, Wittgenstein and Sartre, punsters have long deployed their subversive wit to expose the complex challenges—and perhaps even futility—of defining the world around us. As Oscar Wilde once put it, "Immanuel doesn't pun, he Kant." But of course, he could and did—and with good reason.

Puns also play a formative role in childhood development, by revealing the relationship between words, sounds, context and meaning. Listen carefully, and you'll note that the knock-knock jokes and riddles that children learn on the playground usually turn on puns. For example, what has four wheels and flies? A garbage truck.

It's simple, and not so simple. As children gleefully learn to spot and evaluate secondary meanings in common words and phrases, they're really learning how to think critically. To get the joke, they have to overlook the obvious to explore other possible interpretations of what they have just heard, and fast.

Though often dismissed as juvenile, riddles and knock-knock jokes actually require significant powers of abstraction, a deliberate subversion of rules, and a special appreciation for surprise. Sure, most people abandon those specific forms as they grow older, but many can't shake the underlying impulse to pun.

Perhaps that explains the ubiquity of puns in advertising, pop music, horse racing, literature, Broadway musicals, academia, politics, TV newscasts and daily newspapers. One story about a Middle East peace deal, for example, carried the headline SHEIK ON IT. A back-to-school story was capped with TEACHER STRIKES IDLE KIDS.

Now, it may take us a moment to grasp the secondary meanings, but when we do they're funny. But why? Certainly not because the Arab-Israeli conflict is anything to laugh about, or because the image of teachers hitting students tickles our collective funny bone.

Sometimes the puns we hear are more subtle, but they're even funnier for their clever subversiveness. In 1967, Ronald Reagan, then governor of California, dismissed Clark Kerr as the University of California chancellor, essentially for his refusal to crack down hard enough on antiwar protesters. Upon his farewell, Kerr remarked drily that he was leaving the chancellorship just as he had entered it: "fired with enthusiasm."

So what's the alchemy at work here? How do the best puns manage to layer so much meaning, humor, even irony into just a few words? And why in the world is punning so intrinsic to human expression that it sparks such mischievous delight in languages as diverse as Tzotzil, Yoruba, French, Pitjantjatjara and Japanese?

For that matter, what actually qualifies as a pun? Often, a pun exists only in the mind of the punster and, somewhat less often, in the ear of the listener. And while linguists have defined the pun's principal forms (at least in English), its many variations actually defy easy categorization. In fact, puns appear so often and in such diverse forms and cultures throughout history that they appear to reflect something fundamental, enduring and perhaps even universal about human expression.

From the dawn of recorded history, no civilization has achieved greatness without a mastery of complex language. Whether Egyptian, Sumerian, Phoenician, Chinese, Greek, Roman, Arab, Persian, French or English, the great empires of history have generally triumphed not just through the sword or ship, but through the power of the words they used to persuade, proselytize, trade, govern and—invariably—to pun.

But what, exactly, is the link between punning and civilization? What cultural, emotional or functional need does it fulfill across so many centuries and continents? What makes wordplay in general, and punning specifically, such an enduring part of language? Could it be biological and, if so, what evolutionary purpose might it serve? And why should laughter itself even matter in the survival of the fittest?

Ultimately, while puns may seem simple, the art and implications of punning are not. So why, exactly, *do* bears go barefoot, and what does that reveal about the human condition?

I hope you enjoy this hunt for answers.

# The Pun Also Rises

# CHAPTER 1

# *Cutting It Up:*
# *The Anatomy of a Pun*

ON A DRIZZLING AFTERNOON IN OLD LONDON, IN AN AGE WHEN
men of certain stature or pretention still carried swords about
the city's crowded streets, two scholars sat fireside at the Grecian Coffee-House on Devereux Court, arguing fiercely over
the accent of a Greek word.

It was no mere academic argument. This was a time when
philosophers, writers and scientists were spinning revolutionary ideas—Isaac Newton, among others, was a regular at the
Grecian—and even single words carried gravity. Shifting that
accent could transform the word's very meaning, and on such

*1*

distinctions history turned, at least in the minds of those who earned their living putting quill to paper.

"Those learned pundits who would gather there," one chronicler of the dispute wrote, did not just "discuss the trivialities of the day, but those weightier matters that concern the rise and fall of dynasties, such as the fate of Rome and the events which issued from the Trojan war."

Perhaps the coffee was too strong that day, but tempers soon flared. Honor impugned, the two antagonists determined to settle their dispute outside. Striding out into the darkening bluster of the narrow lane, they drew their blades and began to circle.

"Whatever the accent ought to have been," the chronicler wrote, "the quarrel was *acute*, and its conclusion *grave*." Indeed, the grammar of violence ultimately proved decisive as the quicker scholar—making his final point—ran his rival through, killing him on the spot.

So much for dual interpretations.

This seventeenth-century incident, by all accounts true, may sound extreme. But disputes over language, specifically over origins, pronunciation and meaning, have divided people since the earliest scribes first scratched their marks into the wet clay tablets of ancient Mesopotamia. Carved records from the first millennium BC tell us that the princes of Babylon actually challenged each other to riddling duels whose answers depended on puns, and that such contests could readily escalate to armed conflict.

But evidence suggests that the pun's roots lie even deeper. In his 1929 excavations at the ancient city of Ur, in what is today southern Iraq, the British archeologist Sir Leonard Woolley discovered a thick layer of sediment separating the ruins of mighty civilizations. Along with subsequent discoveries, this geological evidence indicated a massive, destructive deluge in ancient times—one that seemed to corroborate stories of the Great Flood as recounted in the Epic of Gilgamesh in the seventh century BC, and later in Genesis, as the story of Noah's Ark.

In Gilgamesh, angry gods decide to flood the earth. One god warns a mortal under his protection of the coming waters, and urges him to build a vessel and "bring all seed of life in the ship." In order to calm suspicious neighbors as he builds his ark, this chosen one is instructed to assure them that the heavens "would soon rain *kibtu* and *kukku* on them."

Then as now, people tend to hear what they want to hear. *Kibtu* means "corn," and *kukku* means "the sound of corn being ground"—good news in a land whose prosperity flowed from irrigated agriculture. But *kibtu* and *kukku* were also puns on the words for grief and misfortune. And as legend tells it, those who failed to catch history's first corny puns paid with their lives.

## BOMBSHELLS

Sadly, the arc of Mesopotamian history seems stubbornly consistent. Today, many millennia after the Great Flood, grief and misfortune are still raining down along the Euphrates. Yet even as suicide bombers attack and the anguish escalates, New York headline writers who chronicle the mayhem still wield puns without shame, to attract and entertain readers, editorialize and boost newsstand sales.

HOLY SHIITE read one of the paper's irreverent headlines,

poking crude fun at *Newsweek* for having to retract its inflammatory (and inaccurate) story about U.S. interrogators allegedly flushing a Koran down the toilet at Guantanamo Bay, Cuba.

RUMS FELLED proclaimed yet another, topping a photo of Donald Rumsfeld, the fired Defense Secretary, being ushered from the Oval Office one last time. "BUSH SHOWS WAR CHIEF THE DOOR."

And the list grows daily. Incidentally, punning headlines first started appearing in New York newspapers toward the end of the Great Depression. One of the very first rolled off the presses in the January 2, 1940, issue of the *New York Daily News*. It dealt with an incident at a New Year's Eve party in the swank Rainbow Room at Rockefeller Center. It seems that a certain "blonde bombshell" in a white satin dress was doing the conga on the crowded dance floor as midnight approached and started "lifting her dress slightly above a pair of well-turned knees." Ever hopeful, a man yelled out, "Come on baby, go to town!"

And that she did, suddenly whipping the dress up over her head to reveal absolutely nothing, and everything, at once.

"Holy Mackerel!" the second violinist shouted, as the Eddie LeBaron orchestra screeched to a halt, and the entire dance floor turned to stare.

"Keep playing!" someone shouted. The dress, tangled for a moment overhead, tumbled back down like a curtain. The music came up, and the party shimmied on into the night.

The story's headline? AMATEUR STRIP TEASE TITILLATES RAINBOW ROOM. And on the jump page? HAPPY NUDE YEAR.

In bad times and good, far away and close to home, the pun has always crossed and recrossed boundaries of propriety, authority and meaning. And wherever the pun appears, it seems that controversy is never far behind. Modern scholars, in fact, can't even agree on the etymology of the word itself.


## TANGLED ROOTS

The *Oxford English Dictionary* suggests that *pun* is likely seventeenth-century slang clipped from a longer word, perhaps *punnet* or *pundigrion* (much as the word *mob* was clipped from *mobile vulgus*). Pundigrion itself is possibly a perversion of the Italian *puntiglio*, a small or fine point. But for all its musings, the OED ultimately concludes that the word is "of unascertained origin." This shouldn't come entirely as a surprise —puns often seem to appear from nowhere, even to those who make them. Still, the OED is not necessarily QED, and the word's origins might be significantly older. Some etymologists posit that the English word *pundit*—which today generally refers to a political commentator—can be traced to the second millennium BC and means "a learned Hindu versed in Sanskrit."

Sanskrit, one of the earliest Indo-European languages, is a famously complex tongue rich in its use of puns—not for humorous effect, but for the pun's perceived power to reveal divine truth beyond the surface of any given word. In *The Secret Life of Words: How English Became English*, Henry Hitchings writes that Sanskrit itself means synthesized, and suggests that it reflects a process of putting together, allowing "the boundaries between individual words to blur into a fluid yarn of syllables."

"Pundits," he writes, "were required to unpack [Sanskrit's] ambiguities."

Notably, it is ambiguity that gives meaning and power to most puns. And given that English has adapted or adopted a good number of Sanskrit words—*wit, shampoo, jungle, nirvana, bandana* and *pundit*, among others—isn't it plausible that we borrowed *pun*, too?

The timing fits. According to Dr. Terttu Nevalainen, the Director of the Research Unit for Variation, Contacts and Change in English at the University of Helsinki, the earliest surviving record of the word *pundit* in English dates from 1672, almost simultaneously with the first appearance of the word *pun*, as documented by the OED.

This arrival jibes with the rising cultural and commercial impact of Britain's East India Company, which was chartered by Queen Elizabeth in 1600 and began importing exotic goods—along with new language—as fast as its armed merchantmen could sail around the Cape of Good Hope.

Other Sanskrit stowaways of the period include *toddy* in 1609, *guru* and *pariah* in 1612, and *cot* in 1613. Meanwhile, wordplay—especially punning—was enjoying a heyday in England. "All the world's a stage," Shakespeare had written in *As You Like It*, first performed in 1599. The comedy ushered in an entirely new type of dramatic Shakespearian fool, one intended to spark laughs not through buffoonery, but through wit and intellect.

"The truest poetry is the most feigning," asserts Touchstone, the play's jester. To a seventeenth-century audience, the pun would have been clear. *Feign* means "to fake or pretend," while *fain* means "compelled by circumstances." And perhaps those most inclined to play with language found that the existing terms for this type of wordplay—cavil, quibble and clinch—

were not quite as compelling as this playful newcomer from the exotic East, the pun.

Nice theory, but not so fast, says Madhav M. Deshpande, Professor of Sanskrit and Linguistics at the University of Michigan. "The Sanskrit word for pun is *śleṣa* and this is unrelated to the word *paṇḍita*," he writes, adding that *paṇḍita* comes from the word *paṇḍā*, meaning "intellect."

But perhaps the bare facts are not so black and white. Tucked away on the bottom shelf in a quiet corner of the New York Public Library's great reading room sits an obscure, yellowing tome entitled *An Etymological Dictionary of the English Language*, first published in 1879 and authored by one "Elrington and Bosworth Professor of Anglo-Saxon in the University of Cambridge and Fellow of Christ's College, the Rev. Walter W. Skeat, Litt.D., D.C.L., L.L.D., Ph.D., F.F.A."

Completely ignoring purported roots such as *puntiglio* or *pundigrion*, Skeat suggests that to pun is a variation of to pound, explaining that "to *pun* is to pound words, to beat them into new senses, to hammer at forced similes" (a secondary etymology also offered in the OED). And while Skeat confirms that pundit can indeed be traced to the Sanskrit *paṇḍita*, he offers another Sanskrit root as well: *puṇḍ*—to heap up or together. A pun, in its purest form, is a word or phrase containing layered, or multiple, meanings. Given this remarkable similarity of sound and sense, could *puṇḍ* be the long-lost root of pun?

That's probably pounding a little too hard, said Anatoly Liberman, Professor of Humanities at the University of Minnesota, and the author of *Word Origins and How We Know Them*, as well as *An Analytic Dictionary of English Etymology: An Introduction*.

Liberman, who writes an online column on word origins called The Oxford Etymologist, explains that while the aim of etymology is to discover the roots of any given word, modern linguists now dismiss the idea that there was ever a time of "pure roots" in the history of Indo-European languages. "This stage is a mirage, a vision of virile and highly potent stubs," he writes.

For nearly two decades, Liberman has been researching a new etymological dictionary that focuses on English words of unknown origin, *pun* among them. He documents evidence of pun's debut in English sometime about 1640—nearly three decades earlier than the OED's first citation. Liberman cites a 1641 production of *The Guardian*, a comedy by Abraham Cowley, in which a character named Mr. Puny is described as "a young Gallant, a pretender to wit."

Supporting evidence appears in a 1661 revision of the play, in which Cowley used the adjective *punish* in reference to Mr. Puny's wit—an obvious punning connotation.

But that still doesn't help expose the etymological root of the pun. In an effort to do so, Liberman debunks the competing pretenders one by one, including the archaic Scottish *pun* (meaning "sham"), the old English *pun* (meaning "to pound"), its phonetic cousin *fun*, the Irish Gaelic *bun* (meaning "root, or foundation"), the French *pointe* (meaning "point"), the Italian *puntiglio* (meaning "small or fine point"), the conflation of *puzzle* and *conundrum*, as well as the OED's suggested *punnet* and *pundigrion*—this latter a nonsensical word he calls "baffling." Liberman, a proud punster himself, even tosses the Sanskrit *puṇḍ* onto the heap of rejected forebears, too.

"One sometimes wishes for a punitive expedition against the people who offer such hypotheses, but since they are all dead and therefore invulnerable to my slings and arrows, the raid has to be called off," he writes.

As his best educated guess at the root of *pun*, Liberman suggests the Latin *punctilio*, or "fine point." Regretfully, though, he concludes that "the etymology of the pun will remain unresolved."

However, there is one last possibility. In a fascinating 1903 dictionary entitled *Hobson-Jobson: A Glossary of Colloquial Anglo-Indian Words and Phrases, and of Kindred Terms, Etymological, Historical, Geographical and Discursive*, the editors note that a *Pun* is a word for "a stake played for a price, a sum," and as such gives its name to a certain type of Indian coin. Carried back to England in the pockets of a sailor or two, could the Pun, with its two faces, have taken on a new, richer meaning?

In a toss-up, I'd wager it possible.


## DEFINITIONS


If the pun's etymology is difficult to determine, so too is a precise definition. *Webster's* dictionary defines a pun as "the humorous use of a word in such a way as to suggest different meanings or applications or of words having the same or nearly the same sound but different meanings." The *Oxford English Dictionary* defines it almost identically. But such definitions don't capture all forms of what we commonly consider puns, a failure these dictionaries tacitly acknowledge with the additional, much broader definition of "play on words."

But there is a distinction between the two, as Paul Hammond and Patrick Hughes note in *Upon the Pun*, their quirky, 1978 taxonomy of the form. "While the pun emphasizes perception, the play on words emphasizes cognition," they write.

In other words, a pun transforms one thing into another by relating them through sound or, in the case of visual puns, sight. A play on words only works if the two things it relates are already intrinsically connected, either by etymology or function. Three examples illustrate this. "The excitement at the circus is in tents," Hughes and Hammond write, pointing out the two obvious meanings a listener is likely to hear: "in tents" and "intense." This is a homophonic pun—one based on homophones, or words that sound alike but have different meanings.

The next example they give is subtly different: "An architect in prison complained that the walls were not built to scale." In this case, the dual meanings depend on how a listener interprets the word *scale*. Does "scale" refer to a building's relative proportions, as an architect might see them? Or does "scale" refer to the difficulty someone might encounter were they to attempt an escape by climbing over the prison walls?

The circus example is a pure homophonic pun. The prison example, Hammond and Hughes argue, is a mere play on words. The difference is that *intense* and *in tents* are completely unrelated words, except through an accident of sound. By contrast, the alternate meanings of *scale* stem from the same etymological root, the Latin *scala*, meaning "ladder."

A third example Hughes and Hammond offer concerns a cruise director who says that "rumors about sex orgies aboard the ship are all bunk." Unlike the previous wordplay on *scale*, this one is a true pun because *bunk* has two meanings, each deriving from different etymological roots. The first meaning is "a type of stacked bed often found on ships," which the authors trace back to the Old Swedish word *bunke*. The second meaning is "windbaggery or nonsense," and is short for *bunkum*, itself a bastardization of Buncombe County, North Carolina. As the story goes, a long-winded congressman from the area named Felix Walker gave a lengthy and vacuous speech in the House chamber in 1820, apologizing to his colleagues for its emptiness but explaining that his constituents expected him "to make a speech for Buncombe."

To most punsters, such distinctions don't even register, let alone matter. As the polymath writer Arthur Koestler noted, the etymological roots of any given pun are irrelevant "provided the two derivations have drifted apart far enough to become incompatible." And while punning might have once been a life-or-death business to ancient Babylonians and later to a few European hotheads, it has long since entered the realm of humor and, over the past century, serious academic study.

In one particularly rigorous deconstruction of humor entitled *The Linguistic Analysis of Jokes*, artificial intelligence researcher Graeme Ritchie critiques linguists' competing theories of verbal humor and punning, and even offers an appendix of mathematical formulas for certain types of jokes and "linguistically normal" puns. Yet, despite such extensive efforts by such accomplished thinkers to corral the pun within precise definitions, formulas and theories, it always seems to jump the fence.

Still, those holding pens offer us a useful guide to the pun and its penumbra.

Some linguists divide puns into two principal categories: homophonic and homographic. Homophonic puns exploit words that sound alike, either generally or identically, such as "in tents" and "intense." By contrast, homographic puns are based on etymologically distinct words, spelled the same, that have more than one meaning, such as *bunk*.

Others suggest still different categories. One is a paradigmatic pun, which depends on the listener grasping a greater context to "get" the joke, as in "the mother superior forbade the lustful monk from slipping into the convent after midnight, but he would have none of it." In this case, the pun on *none* requires knowledge of the implied word and meaning of "nun," which appears nowhere in the joke.

Another common category is the more self-contained, or syntagmatic, pun. In this type of pun, all the information necessary to get the joke is provided within sequential use of similar or identical words, as in "The wedding was beautiful. The bride was in tears, and the cake was in tiers, too."

Complicating matters, these four categories of puns can overlap, and their offspring multiply fast. Consider the Spoonerism, in which a speaker transposes words or parts of words to create a phrase that still makes sense, but in an odd or funny way. It was named for the Reverend Archibald Spooner, who led Oxford's New College in the early twentieth century, and who suffered from an inadvertent tendency to jumble his words. According to more than one account, Spooner, an avid oarsman in his college days, was walking along the riverbank when he spotted an amorous couple out in a punt, kissing. "Young man," he shouted, "cunts are not for pissing in!" Other stories record him welcoming Queen Victoria with a similarly embarrassing slip of the tongue: Intending to express a "half-formed wish," Spooner instead told the queen of his "half-warmed fish . . ."

While some Spooner scholars suggest that these specific examples are likely apocryphal, they acknowledge that Spooner did earn his reputation for similar, unintentional transpositions. In one well-documented instance, Spooner, a minister who spoke often from the pulpit, explained that Noah's flood "was barrowed from Bobylon." When baptizing twins named Kate and Sydney, he called them "Steak and Kidney." And once, while performing wedding rites, he pronounced the happy couple "loifully jawned in holy matrimony." This last specimen was so ripe with possibility that a local wag quickly polished it for posterity as "loinfully jawed in holy matrimony."

Spooner first arrived at Oxford as an undergraduate in 1862, and never left. And over the ensuing fifty-eight years, he earned a reputation around town as a friendly, modest, self-effacing scholar and administrator, albeit a little hapless and confused. According to biographer William Hayter, Spooner was embarrassed by his penchant for verbal blunders, and studiously tried to avoid the so-called Spoonerisms that had, by the mid-1880s, already come to bear his name.

It's a documented fact that Spoonerisms, a type of transposition formally known as metathesis, existed long before Spooner. A few decades earlier, medical students in London had called them Marrowskys, supposedly after an eighteenth-century Polish count who was said to suffer the same tendency. But it was Spooner who made them famous.

According to Hayter, one reason that Spoonerisms spread so widely is that campus mischief makers (including one appropriately named W. W. Merry, Rector of Lincoln College) contrived and disseminated increasingly elaborate examples under Spooner's name, which were in turn propagated by the popular press in both Britain and the United States. With his reputation spreading as fast as the telegraph, telephone and finally radio could transmit, Spooner became something of a minor celebrity.

Michael Erard, in *Um . . . Slips, Stumbles and Verbal Blunders, and What They Mean*, suggests that other, societal factors contributed to Spooner's fame, too. Among them was a rising awareness of human errors and their potential impact in a technological age, when management of increasingly complex systems such as railroads could have life-or-death consequences. Citing an 1889 article in *Scribner's*, Erard tells of a horrific train accident that resulted when a train's engineer thought one thing (applying the brake) but did the opposite, killing twelve.

Another factor that may have advanced the popularity of Spoonerisms was a rising public awareness of the subconscious, due in large part to the contemporaneous work of psychologist Sigmund Freud. In 1905, Freud published "Jokes and Their Relation to the Unconscious," which suggested that slips of the tongue could offer vital clues to repressed thoughts. In that context, just about anybody's slips, including Spooner's, offered curious listeners endless fodder for psychological speculation.

Spooner died in 1930. But by then his reputation for Spoonerisms had been firmly established. Punning away, the British humor magazine *Punch* had long since dubbed him "Oxford's great metaphasiarch." Others, too, had turned "the Spoo," as he was nicknamed, into spoof. Even professional comedians were now aggressively using Spoonerisms in pursuit of a deliberate laugh, including one William Claude Dukenfield, better known as W. C. Fields.

"I'd rather have a bottle in front of me than a frontal lobotomy," Fields once said. Or is said to have said. That Spoonerism, like so many others, is of disputed origin. Depending on the source one consults, Dorothy Parker, Dean Martin and others are also credited with the joke.

## FRIENDS, ROMANS, COMEDIANS

Such clever Spoonerisms are not the only jokes of disputed provenance. In *Stop Me If You've Heard This: A History and Phi-*

*losophy of Jokes,* Jim Holt cites compelling evidence that the Western world has been recycling the same jokes over and over for at least 2,500 years, variously covering the topics of booze, sex, marriage, money, bad breath, big talkers and *scholastikos*— the absent-minded professor, or egghead.

Holt notes that jokes were popular enough in the ancient world that Athens featured a famous comedians' club called the Group of Sixty, whose jokes were so funny that Philip of Macedon (father of Alexander the Great) supposedly paid scribes to record them for posterity. But that collection, lost to history, wasn't even the first known joke book. That honor belongs to the *Philogelos,* a set of 264 Greek jokes first compiled in the fourth or fifth century BC.

A few centuries later, Marcus Tullius Cicero—the Roman philosopher, orator and celebrated wit——published history's first dedicated pun book, recording a selection of his favorites. Known for his sharp tongue, Cicero criticized the Greek rhetoricians, who were at that time not so ancient, for their failure to formulate rules governing the use of humor. One rule he did practice, however, was to claim authorship of the best puns making their way around Rome and disavow the rest.

While the jokes from the *Philogelos* were already old in Cicero's day, many of them have nonetheless survived for millennia. Not all jokes that rely on Greek puns will strike the modern reader as funny, however. Holt recounts one about a boy who asks his father about the volume of a standard five-liter flask. The punch line is only humorous if you know that the ancient Greek word for that flask was also a pun on penis.

This leads us back, in a roundabout way, to the Spoonerism. A cross-cultural phenomenon, it found earlier and saucier expression in the old French tradition of *contrepèterie.* First recorded in the sixteenth century, this type of wordplay involves rearranging phonemes (the distinct building blocks of sound that differentiate words) to form amusing sentences, often double entendres alluding to sexual content.

In the centuries since it was first popularized by satirist François Rabelais in his novels *La vie de Gargantua et de Pantagruel,* many French literary figures including Hugo, Balzac and others have embraced the subversive *contrepèterie*, too. And as fate would have it, their humor ultimately became a matter of life or death. Before the Allied invasion of Normandy, derring-do members of the French Resistance regularly tuned in to Radio London for coded messages broadcast by Colonel Rémy, the French spymaster. Then, using a popular 1934 treasury of *contrepèterie*, they decoded his instructions and set to work blowing up designated bridges, rescuing downed airmen and otherwise undermining Nazi occupiers.

ANOTHER CLOSE COUSIN OF THESE TRANSPOSITIONAL PUNS IS the chiasmus, derived from the Greek word for cross-wise arrangement. A chiasmus simply reverses the order of words in similar phrases to give them different meanings. For instance, an epitaph to a nineteenth-century musician summed up his life as follows: "Stephen beat time, now time beats Stephen." In a different context, movie star Mae West once quipped that "it's not the men in my life that count—it's the life in my men."

Grammatical sticklers might insist that such chiasma are technically just wordplay, not true puns. They are in the minority and, in any case, miss the larger point. Punning is all about connecting ideas, no matter how disparate. And like the law, its rules offer widest latitude to advocates who can make the jury laugh.

Another type of common pun is the Wellerism, although not all Wellerisms constitute a pun. Named for the fictional Sam Weller in Charles Dickens's *The Pickwick Papers*, a punning Wellerism forces the listener to reconsider the meaning of a simple phrase by cleverly deploying the word *as*. A familiar example would be: "'I see,' said the blind man, as he picked up his hammer and saw." Is the blind man speaking of a sudden insight while picking a hammer and saw? Or is he picking up the hammer and then recovering his sight? Without additional context, it's impossible to nail down one definitive meaning, because both lie within the same construction.

When Charles Dickens first published *The Pickwick Papers* in 1836 as a serial, it met with little success. Only when he introduced the streetwise Weller did the novel take off, jumping from five hundred to forty thousand copies per month and making Dickens a bestselling author.

As the folklorist Florence Baer notes, however, Dickens did not actually invent the Wellerism: Scholars have identified the same or similar structures in classical Greek, Italian, German, Dutch, Spanish, Swedish, Hebrew and various African cultures. But original or not, and fanned by newspaper editors looking to entertain growing audiences, Wellerisms became a fad in both England and then the United States, where patriots who could still remember the War of 1812 insisted on calling them Yankeeisms.

A close cousin of the Wellerism is also named after a fictional character, Tom Swift. Swift was the youthful protagonist of a series of more than one hundred science fiction adventure books that bear his name, published almost continuously for the past century. Tom Swift's creator, Edward Stratemeyer, instructed his team of ghostwriters to avoid endless repetition of the word *said* in sentence after sentence, book after book. So, to vary their prose, they made liberal use of other verbs and adverbs. Eventually, as the books became more and more popular, this style lent itself to punning parody, examples of which became known as "Tom Swifties."

"My shirt needs pressing," the bare-chested man observed ironically.

"I definitely need another load of mulch," the gardener repeated.

"I absolutely love ribbons," the beauty queen said with abandon.

"Next time, I should probably use a chair to fend off Leo," the lion tamer sighed off-handedly.

The formula worked. Between 1910 and 1941, when the first Tom Swift series was published, Stratemeyer sold 30 million copies. Add that to his popular Nancy Drew, Hardy Boys, Rover Boys and Bobsey Twins series, and his total sales over the twentieth century topped 200 million books.

But let us move on, swiftly, to yet another type of pun.

This type's roots stretch back some eight hundred years when, on a violently stormy night, a knight struggled through the downpour, leading his lame horse by the bridle. The mud sucked hungrily at his sodden leather boots, the forest was thick, and the path itself was revealed only by the occasional flash of lightning.

After what seemed an eternity of trudging, the knight saw a warm glow in the distance; it was the window of a small inn, flickering with the firelight within. He coaxed his injured horse onward, and soon they arrived. After tying his mount to a large tree, the knight began pounding on the door, but the thunder was so loud that nobody inside seemed to hear.

Finally, a stooped innkeeper opened the door and ushered the bedraggled knight inside, to dry off by the hearth. After a short rest and a tankard of hot mead, the knight explained that he was on an urgent mission for the king. Could the innkeeper loan him a horse to press onward through the night?

The innkeeper shook his head, explaining that he had no horses in the stable. But in the morning, if the storm broke, he could talk to a nearby farmer, and perhaps secure a mount. The knight, determined to continue his journey without delay, suddenly got an idea. At his feet, in front of the fireplace, lay an extraordinarily large shaggy dog, snoring away beside a half-chewed bone. The dog was huge, almost as big as a Shetland pony.

"Since you have no horses," he said to the innkeeper, "might I borrow your dog to ride onward?"

The innkeeper paused, glancing out the rain-spattered window just as another bolt of lightning slashed the darkness.

"No sir," he said. "I just couldn't put a knight out on a dog like this."

Like most story puns, this example involves a setup narrative whose punch line is a punning adaptation of a common proverb or saying—in this case, "I just couldn't put a dog out on a night like this." The more elaborate the setup, the more it qualifies as a "shaggy dog" story. But not all shaggy dog stories involve puns or even shaggy dogs. In this particular case, the appearance of a shaggy dog, as opposed to a short-haired one, was sheerly gratuitous.

Some story puns (which are occasionally called a Feghoot, for their frequent use in the science fiction series "Through Time and Space with Ferdinand Feghoot") are more modest in their setup. Sometimes, their punch lines play off a single word. As the story goes, Mahatma Gandhi was known for walking hundreds of miles barefoot. Over time, he developed incredibly thick calluses on his feet, stronger than the soles of many boots. He also ate lightly and fasted often, which left him frail and gave him chronically bad breath.

And do you know what this made him? A super-calloused fragile mystic hexed by halitosis.

The punch line is only humorous to the listener who hasn't heard the joke before, and who's already familiar with the tongue-twisting song "Supercalifragilisticexpialidocious," popularized by Julie Andrews and Dick van Dyke in the 1964 film version of *Mary Poppins*. Like the knight's tale, it's an example of a paradigmatic pun—one requiring outside context to get the joke.

Curiously, the shaggy dog story itself is something of a mutt as humor goes. According to researchers at Indiana University's Folklore Archives, there are more than two hundred types and subtypes of the genre, many of which overlap. At the peak of the shaggy dog craze in the early 1950s, the noted lexicographer Eric Partridge even devoted an entire book to the subject. In *The 'Shaggy Dog' Story—Its Origin, Development and Nature (with a few seemly examples)*, Partridge traces the form to ancient Greece, where the dramatists had a special word for it, roughly translated as "sudden unexpectedness."

But the earliest description of a "shaggy dog" story by that name doesn't appear until 1943, and likely references a popular Depression-era tale of an American who became so moved reading an article about an Englishman's grief over his lost dog that he decides to find the man an identical dog, based on the newspaper photo, and present it to him as a gift. After exhaustive efforts to locate and purchase just the right dog—including the proper pedigree, sex, age, size, color and temperament—he boards a ship in New York, bound for England.

It's a stormy passage, and both he and the dog are miserable. But after docking in Southampton and taking the train to London, they regain top form. After a few days of inquiries, the American finally manages to locate the Englishman's address and arrives at his doorstep with the dog. It's an imposing brick town house in a posh neighborhood. Walking up the front steps, he notices that the brass knocker on the door is a dog's face—one indistinguishable from the dog he's brought.

With great anticipation, the American knocks. The dog, who's exceptionally well-trained, sits at his side, softly thumping his tail. After a short wait, a uniformed butler opens the door. Smiling, the American quickly explains the personal mission that's brought him across the ocean, motions to the dog, and asks if he might present it to the master of the house. The butler, squinting ever so briefly at the dog, firmly declines and starts to shut the door.

The American, crestfallen, interjects. "But why?" he asks. "What's wrong with the dog?"

The butler is unapologetic. "I'm afraid that this dog is just a bit too shaggy."

One final, relatively short example of this genre is in order, slightly adapted from the esteemed Random House publisher Bennett Cerf's *Treasury of Atrocious Puns*. As the story goes, a Mr. Smith had just supervised the pouring of a fine new walkway outside his home and was outraged when—looking out his window a short while later—he spied his three boys pressing their hands and footprints into the wet concrete. Running out the door in a fury, he chased his children, yelling wildly. Not surprisingly, they scattered, and he couldn't catch them.

Still angry, he stomped back into the house, red-faced and sweaty. At dinnertime, hungry and contrite, the boys finally returned home to accept their punishment. Without mercy, he walloped all three.

"You brute!" his wife said. "Don't you love your children at all?"

"In the abstract, yes. But not in the concrete!"

THIS BRINGS US TO THE DOORSTEP OF THE KNOCK-KNOCK joke, which many English-speaking children begin learning at the age of three or four. The basic format is well-known:

> Knock-Knock!
> Who's there?
> Isabelle.
> Isabelle who?
> Isabelle necessary on a bicycle?

According to artificial intelligence researchers at the University of Cincinnati, there are three types of knock-knock jokes. The simplest type appears above, in which the punch line plays directly off the sound of the knocker's given name. In this case the name Isabelle sounds exactly like "Is a bell . . ."

A second type requires the listener to recognize and compensate for a slight phonetic gap between the knocker's given name and a distinct but similar-sounding word with a different meaning, as in the following:

> Knock-knock!
> Who's there?
> Max.

Max who?
Max no difference.

In the third type, the punch line depends on a play off the phonetics of the doorkeeper's request for a last name.

Knock-knock!
Who's there?
Tank.
Tank who?
You're welcome.

And the list goes on, as mischievous knockers stretch and break the format. While some critics might dismiss the genre as juvenile, the linguistics involved are actually quite complex. As the researchers at the University of Cincinnati discovered, a specially programmed computer was reasonably successful in identifying the existence of wordplay in knock-knock jokes, but struggled to identify whether punch lines actually worked or not. In other words, even talented programmers had trouble encoding the subtle rules describing what makes something humorous.

Some knock-knock jokes get recycled, generation after generation. Few recognize, however, how old the knock-knock joke actually is. Literary evidence suggests that the form dates back to the early seventeenth century. One example from 1605 appears in Shakespeare's *Macbeth*. In Act II, Scene 3, the porter plays both roles: "Knock, knock! Who's there? Faith, here's an English tailor come hither, for stealing out of a French hose."

He answers his own question: "Come in, tailor; here you may roast your goose."

While the humor may not seem obvious to a modern listener, the answer includes at least one pun. Scholars suggest
that the porter's invitation to "roast your goose" is really a double entendre (from the French, meaning "understood two
ways"). The porter is suggesting that the dishonest tailor warm
his seam-sealing iron with the heat of hell, because he's been
trying to cheat customers on fabric, even as changing fashions
dictated tighter and tighter pants in the French style ("stealing
out of a French hose").

Knock-knock jokes are not just limited to English. Variants
of the form exist in Japan (*Kon-Kon*), in France (*Toc-Toc*), and
in the Netherlands (*Klop-Klop*), among others.

Which leads us to the bilingual pun. In a paper entitled
"Better than the Original: Humorous Translations that Succeed," Arizona State University English Professor Don Nilsen
notes that words in one language often sound the same as
words in another, but with completely different meanings.
This gives rise to rich opportunities for punning, as long as the
audience knows both languages.

> "Knock-knock."
> "Who's there?"
> "Kelly."
> "Kelly who?"
> "Kelly importa?!"

To a Spanish-speaker, the punch line sounds like "*Que le
importa?!*" Retranslated into English, it becomes, roughly,
"What's it to you?!"

In a similar spirit, Nilsen offers the following riddle:

"How do you kill a Polish herring?"
"With a sledge hammer."

Unsuspecting listeners might lodge a complaint, asking why they should consider this humorous. It's because the Polish word for herring is *shledzh*.

Riddles in general are often rich with wordplay and constitute another major genre of punning. In *No Laughing Matter: An Analysis of Sexual Humor*, Gershon Legman, the noted scholar of the dirty joke, posed the following:

> A girl is standing on a street corner and three men go by, one on a horse, one on a bicycle, and one on foot. One of the men knows the girl. Which one?
> The horse manure.

This riddle is actually not so dirty as dirty jokes go, unless you step on the punch line. But Legman goes on to place this one in a meta-context, illustrating the nuance that gives many jokes and puns the breath of life. As he recounts it, an Englishman carried this joke back with him to Great Britain, only to bungle the retelling.

> "A young lady is standing at an intersection—this is in America, you know—and three gentlemen pass by: an equestrian, a pedestrian and a velocipedist. One of them is acquainted with the young lady. Now, which one?"
> His listeners, perplexed, finally give up and request the answer.

The Englishman, suddenly flustered, turned red in the face. "Well, I don't know how that American chap did it," he said. "But the answer is horseshit!"

ANOTHER CATEGORY OF PUNS IS THE SO-CALLED DAFFYNITION, in which daffy definitions give everyday words new meaning. Every year, *The Washington Post* runs a popular neologism contest that recognizes the very best. Some winning submissions in recent years have included the following:

> Flabbergasted—appalled at how much weight you've gained.

> Abdicate—to give up all hope of ever having a flat stomach.

> Balderdash—a rapidly receding hairline.

> Rectitude—the formal, dignified bearing adopted by proctologists.

But perhaps we've stooped too far.

To fully understand the anatomy of a pun, two final types deserve explanation: the meld pun and the portmanteau. The difference between the two is slight. A meld pun overlaps two words in their entirety to create a new one conveying both ideas; superimpose "alcohol" and "holiday," and it forms *alcoholiday*. They flow together easily.

Closely related is the portmanteau, named for a traditional type of French trunk or suitcase that opens like a book, revealing two equal compartments. As a form of punning, the portmanteau combines parts of two or more words to create a unique hybrid, such as *smog* (from "smoke" and "fog"), *brunch* (combining "breakfast" and "lunch") or the belly-busting Thanksgiving novelty known as the turducken.

## RUFFLED FEATHERS

For those unfamiliar with the turducken, the dish is no paltry undertaking. Layered like a Russian nesting doll, it requires inserting a deboned chicken into a deboned duck into a partially deboned turkey, interstitially layered (in some cases) with sausage or cornbread-and-oyster stuffing. The big bird is then variously roasted, grilled or deep-fried, often in conjunction with the above mentioned alcoholiday.

Like the pun itself, the turducken's provenance is disputed; food historians trace it well beyond the American South, all the way back to Rome's Bacchanalian feasts. A more documented forebear was described by the flamboyant French gourmand and father of modern culinary criticism, Alexandre Balthazar Laurent Grimod de La Reynière. In eight volumes between 1803 and 1812, he published the groundbreaking *L'Almanach des gourmands*, a compendium of recipes, restaurant reviews, gourmet shopping tips and food commentary. Among the dishes he detailed was the extraordinary *rôti sans pareil*, or roast without equal.

Summarizing Grimod's seven pages of instructions, the cook was to grasp a dressed garden warbler and gently tuck the tiny bird inside the slightly larger Ortolan bunting, then place that nesting pair inside a lark. Next, layer by layer, the birds were to be inserted successively into a thrush, quail, lapwing, plover, partridge, woodcock, teal, guinea fowl, duck, chicken, pheasant, goose, turkey and ultimately a bustard—the latter a large, somewhat distant relative of the crane. Cooking time varied, but just given the preparation, this thirty-pound flight of fancy never took off, though Grimod's reputation as a gourmand did.

Actually, Grimod was already something of a celebrity in France, having spent decades as a lawyer, theater critic, satirist, practical joker and flamboyant man about town. He was also an unapologetic punster, one who was never afraid to cut, amuse or subvert—often all at once.

Toward this end, his food writing was often salted with social and political commentary. Correctly anticipating that government censors would identify mandatory *redactions*, he wove the offending language throughout the section on port wine *reductions* and left the corresponding gaps in the final edition, just to show readers he was getting the last laugh.

In another mischievous wink, Grimod gave one Almanach essay the punning title *"Des Taches Gourmandes."* In the opening paragraph, he emphasizes that he meant *taches* in the sense of "stains," not *tâches* meaning "arduous tasks." Why? Because "the only task a real gourmand faces is making it through all the courses that precede dessert."

And for a gourmand with less determination than Grimod, that might actually have been the case. Born with severely deformed hands, he wrote, cooked and ate using metal prostheses, often covered with leather gloves. His handicap, and his flamboyant personality, horrified his aristocratic mother, who had married Grimod's father for his money and courted high society with singular determination. According to Grimod biographer Giles MacDonogh, she was so concerned about his deformity's impact on her standing (in her mind a potentially embarrassing sign of dubious lineage) that she actually canceled his public christening and invented a story about his having fallen into a pigpen, where ravenous hogs had eaten his hands.

Despite overcoming his disability with great élan, Grimod never received his mother's love. In actuality, according to Mac-Donogh, his eventual, provocative public persona only infuriated her. One day she happened upon him in the kitchen of their luxurious Paris hôtel, peeling vegetables. Seeing him wield his prostheses so adeptly—and for servants' work, no less—made her doubly furious. Clearly, he was taunting her. But her demeaning protests met with a cutting response. "*Madame ma mère*," Grimod said, "the great difference between a lettuce and the greater part of the people we know, is that à lettuce has a heart."

Sometimes he responded much more forcefully. As a young man, Grimod was known around Paris for wearing a mechanical wig that would tip politely, and apparently automatically, as ladies passed. To some eyes, however, it made him look like a hedgehog and inspired the composition of a popular song that punned on Grimod and *grimaude*, an archaic French word for "slovenly woman."

In the end, though, Grimod's novelty wig sparked more than just amusement. One evening at the opera, according to MacDonogh, a man—perhaps angry over a woman—shoved Grimod roughly. Insults followed and escalated until Grimod's antagonist, an officer of minor nobility, demeaned Grimod's wig and deformity at once. "Give me your address," the man snarled, using the informal *tu* for added offense. "I'll be round tomorrow to comb your hair for you."

It was an affront that no man of honor could brush off, and a duel was promptly arranged for the following day at the Champs-Élysées. At the appointed hour, the men and their seconds arrived, loaded their pistols, and paced off the agreed distance. When the smoke cleared, Grimod's antagonist lay on the ground, a bullet through his eye.

For a night at the opera, death was a high price to pay.

# CHAPTER 2

# Labs and Retrievers: How the Brain Fetches Meaning from Sound

IN 1929, A PROMINENT NEUROSURGEON NAMED OTFRID FOER-ster began a long day of brain surgery on a man in Breslau, known today as the Polish city of Wroclaw. At the time, the city was a center of groundbreaking research in neurology and neuroscience, where top practitioners from around the world would come to observe Foerster and his innovative techniques. One such approach was his pioneering use of local anesthesia, which enabled him to operate on patients while keeping them conscious. This let him probe different parts of the brain to discover which areas governed which functions. In other words, as Foerster opened up the man's skull that day, the patient was still awake.

As recounted by Arthur Koestler in *The Act of Creation*, his wide-ranging book on human creativity, Foerster was seeking to remove a tumor from a man's third ventricle—a small fluid-filled cavity in the middle of the brain adjacent to an area that influences emotions, especially fear. When the surgeon began probing the tumor, the patient "burst into a manic flight of speech" while punning in Latin, Greek, German and Hebrew—much of it apparently related to anxiety about his surgery. Koestler described it as "a gruesome kind of humor coming from a man tied face down to the operating table with his skull open." Koestler went on to note that "the patient's apparently delirious punning and babbling convey a meaningful message to the surgeon—his fear of being butchered, and his entreaty that the surgeon should proceed by careful measurements, that is, in a more cautious, circumspect way."

The incident revealed something else, too: dual systems of governance at work in the patient's brain simultaneously. The first recognized legitimate fears; and the second expressed them through somewhat nonsensical, compulsive, alliterative and assonant puns. Koestler likened such a layered, mysterious process to that of a poet or any creative person who has learned to let the unconscious do its creative work unmolested "while other processes continue simultaneously on the rational surface."

Available accounts do not record if Foerster found his patient's puns amusing or not. But as a deft surgeon, he managed to cut off the stream of humor altogether and still leave the man in stitches. Initially dubbed Foerster's Syndrome, this compulsive punning was later subsumed under the more general term *Witzelsucht*.

*Witzelsucht*, derived from the German words for "wit" and "obsession," describes a medical condition "marked by the making of poor jokes and puns and the telling of pointless stories at which the speaker is intensely amused; a condition characteristic of frontal lobe lesions." This is not to say that all compulsive punsters suffer from lesions, of course.

The existence of such neurological architecture and its abnormalities, however, raises several fundamental questions. What is the biological basis of punning, and from a physiological standpoint, how does the mind actually process sound and associate it with meaning?

Not surprisingly, it's complicated. "Language," writes Harvard psychologist and linguist Steven Pinker, "is not a cultural artifact that we learn the way we learn to tell time or how the federal government works. Instead, it is a distinct piece of the biological makeup of our brains." Pinker encourages people to think of language as an instinct, much as Charles Darwin first identified language acquisition (in some form or another) to be an instinct in other species, such as songbirds.

But how does that instinct actually work? And what evolutionary advantage has language, and therefore punning, offered people in our hardscrabble ascent from creepy crawly to cave dweller to cosmopolitan?

## GETTING A SOUND EDUCATION

To begin answering these questions, it's helpful to quickly review the basics of how sound waves—the physical vibrations that oscillate our eardrums—are conveyed and translated into the neurological signals that flow through the human brain and ultimately become what we interpret as "meaning."

Sound is produced by the physical vibration of matter, whether that vibration takes place through rock, water, air or any other medium with mass and elasticity. When waves of vibrating air arrive at the human ear, they are captured, re-shaped and redirected inward by the auricle—the irregular cuplike structure protruding from either side of the human head.

Traveling through the ear canal, the sound waves begin vibrating the tympanic membrane, a very thin skinlike structure stretched tautly over an opening about the size of a pea. This is the eardrum, and it's extremely sensitive to even slight vibrations. To amplify these vibrations, the human ear employs a sequence of three tiny bones that work like a piston to leverage, concentrate and amplify vibrations, which push on the fluid within a snail-like tube in the inner ear called the cochlea. This is no small feat of biology; without focusing the sound from the tympanic membrane into the millimeter-size opening of the inner ear, most of the sound energy would be lost. The system is so sensitive that it can detect vibrations as slight as that of a single hydrogen atom.

These three little ear bones are common (with some variation in design) to all mammals. It's no coincidence: They give us a competitive advantage, allowing us to pick up extremely faint sounds. Significantly, these bones also allow us to hear while eating. Reptiles, whose jaws and ears are structured differently, lack this capacity. Paleontologists believe that this adaptation helped early mammals coexist with dinosaurs and, over tens of millions of years, made our own, continued evolution possible.

As this fluid is pumped through the cochlea, it passes thousands of microscopic, hairlike vibrating structures called cilia, which are themselves mounted on thousands of hair cells. Because these hairs vary in length and location, they oscillate slightly differently in response to waves of passing fluid. As an analogy, picture a series of ocean waves, driven by wind at the surface, passing through a bed of kelp that's anchored to the sea floor. While every strand is unique in size and location and sways slightly differently, together their movement constitutes a larger, coherent pattern.

As sound waves—in most cases, air compression and expansion—impact the tympanic membrane, the moving cilia create a complex, shifting pattern of stimulation that varies over time and location. Within the cochlea, however, all these tiny hairs don't just bend with the passing current; they act as electrical switches, sending thousands of signals to the brain for interpretation, via the auditory nerve. Each of the cilia within the cochlea is "hardwired" to specific fibers in the auditory nerve, which means that each sound generates a unique pattern of electrical signals. So, depending on what made the noise, where, and when, the brain gets a different set of cues to interpret.

## AN EDUCATED GUESS

But what happens, biologically, when two words have an identical sound but different meanings? Or if we're reading headlines and pronouncing them silently, how do we differentiate between the sound and meaning of words with identical spellings but multiple meanings? Consider the following headlines, which Steven Pinker offers as evidence that words and thoughts are not the same thing.

STUD TIRES OUT

CHILD'S STOOL GREAT FOR USE IN GARDEN

In the first example, are the headline writers talking about obsolete snow tires, an exhausted stallion, or some aging, pot-bellied barfly who finally quits the scene? In the second headline, are we supposed to interpret the word *stool* as something to sit on, or as a kind of fertilizer? Without knowing more context, guessing is something of a crapshoot.

But guessing is what the brain does . . . sort of.

Pinker explains that "when it comes to communicating a thought to someone else, attention spans are short and mouths are slow. To get information into a listener's head in a reasonable amount of time, a speaker can encode only a fraction of the message into words and must count on the listener to fill in the rest. But *inside a single head*, the demands are different."

"Nothing can be left to the imagination," Pinker writes, "because the internal representations *are* the imagination." He suggests that people don't actually think in specific languages per se—whether that's Bulgarian, Mandarin or Finnish—but rather in "a language of thought" he calls mentalese.

As explained by Pinker, a given word might have several corresponding "concept symbols" in mentalese. To an English speaker, for example, the word *stool* could evoke images of a seat, a bowel movement, a wooden duck decoy or, to a naturalist, a root or stump from which new shoots grow. And in each of these cases, that particular "stool" could be envisioned in an infinite variety of colors, shapes and forms—all requiring a unique, more detailed description. As such, Pinker says that knowing a language "is knowing how to translate mentalese into strings of words and vice versa."

This fluid capacity to translate between symbols and words is also the essence of punning, and the best punsters do it with just that, a remarkable mental ease. This ability is a testament to the brain's tremendous computing power, because the tasks involved are complex. On the most basic level, our ability to use language requires the brain to process a stream of sounds, subdivide that stream into discrete segments associated with words of a given language, then associate those words with the relevant concepts in mentalese for interpretation. Often, we then reverse that process to generate sounds that keep the conversation going, all at a remarkable speed.

Quantitatively, the complex communication this makes possible is infinite in variety. According to linguist Noam Chomsky, just about every sentence we say or hear is a recombination of existing words appearing in that exact configuration for the very first time. And it's that profusion of possibility that probably makes punning ubiquitous across so many diverse cultures.

"Languages have a limited array of sound options and an extremely rich array of meanings, so it's going to be almost inevitable that sound sequences are going to be interpretable in many different ways, with all kinds of associations," he said. "If we had to express every concept with a different word, without this kind of overlap or association or suggestiveness, we'd have to construct complicated phrases for simple concepts." Put another way, not to pun at all would be more challenging than most people might imagine.

Chomsky (who describes himself as only an occasional and inadvertent punster) theorizes that all human languages share a deep, underlying universal grammar—one that flows from a genetic, human predisposition to learn and process language. It is this innate biological ability, he argues, that enables children to master the language of their surrounding culture with remarkable speed and uniformity, perhaps by learning what they cannot say, rather than what they can.

While Chomsky is perhaps the world's most renowned linguist, he has his share of critics, too. In one highly publicized research project in the 1970s, a Columbia University psychologist, out to prove that humans aren't alone in their ability to master language as we know it, named his test chimpanzee "Nim Chimpsky" and raised him in a human environment. Despite years of one-on-one instruction in sign language, Nim proved to be a student of limited capacity when it came to mastering language. Subsequent studies suggest that Nim was no numbskull; research indicates that while nonhuman primates communicate a great deal, they do so in ways other than what most experts would generally define as speech.

As brain-imaging technology advanced, many language researchers shifted their focus from animal behavior to the function of the human brain itself, and how it generates electrical signals during thought. In some circles, the brain's convoluted canyons, or sulci, are widely considered to be the ultimate intellectual frontier. With the right equipment, scientists can now track brain signals in action, thereby identifying the brain's principal areas and their corresponding functions.

So just how does the brain process sound-related data once the auditory nerve sends this information, now in the form of electrical signals, onward for analysis? To understand this, we need to take a quick layman's tour of brain anatomy.

## GO FIGURE

At first glance, the brain looks something like a cauliflower, a vegetable Mark Twain once dismissed as "nothing but a cabbage with a college education." The largest part of this "cauliflower" is called the cerebrum, and is divided into two halves: the left and right cerebral hemispheres. Each hemisphere has multiple lobes and complex, layered connections between them. The cerebrum, as a whole, is linked to the spinal cord via the brain stem. Immediately behind the brain stem is the cerebellum, a structure that helps govern the body's movement.

The left and right hemispheres each take the lead in processing different types of information, although both can be engaged simultaneously or in quick succession to solve a problem. Language is commonly, but not exclusively, processed by the left hemisphere by a majority of people, especially if they're right-handed. Generally speaking, the left hemisphere also dominates in organization, calculation and other analytical tasks, while the right hemisphere dominates in recognition, patterns, emotions, music and creativity.

These tendencies are a principal reason why people often overgeneralize in describing "left-brained" and "right-brained" people, depending on whether they're more analytical or creative. In reality, every person is different, and our brains often improvise, as necessary. Much like a traffic detour along the service road beside an interstate keeps traffic flowing around an accident, the brain will sometimes recruit other parts of the brain for specific tasks if the area that normally handles that job gets damaged.

Most of this brain traffic, healthy or otherwise, consists of specialized messenger cells, called neurons, which transmit electrical and chemical signals to other cells throughout the brain, muscles and other parts of the body. In the case of sound, the electrical signals generated by the compression of fluid in the cochlea activate millions of designated language neurons that, in a relay of extraordinary speed, transfer the data to various destinations throughout the brain.

But where?

Not surprisingly, to multiple destinations, much like a general contractor might start phoning his most trusted subcontractors to tackle a complex building project. As a subset of language, puns tend to activate the left hemisphere first, especially the frontal lobe. But within a fraction of a second, the right hemisphere springs into action, too, searching for relevant background information to help the listener establish context. At least two other nearby structures also get to work, especially if the listener is contemplating and preparing a verbal response: the cerebellum, which helps integrate language and emotions with motor control, and the thalamus, which (among other functions) processes and relays auditory signals.

Recalling the case of the surgeon Otfrid Foerster and his manically punning patient, the tumor he was manipulating was located on the floor of the patient's third ventricle, immediately adjacent to the thalamus. The puns burst forth whenever he pressed on the tumor, presumably as it in turn pressured the thalamus.

Nowadays, thanks to functional Magnetic Resonance Imaging (fMRI), brain researchers don't need to cut someone's skull open to watch the brain at work or at play. And in 2005, researchers from the University of California at San Diego and the University of Ghent published a fascinating paper entitled "Hemispheric asymmetry and pun comprehension: When cowboys have sore calves."

In a series of experiments, the researchers wired groups of healthy native English speakers, both men and women, with twenty-nine electrodes to measure brain activity, as well as instruments to measure eye movement. This equipment allowed them to track N400 brain waves, which are electrical signals of a certain frequency, amplitude and pattern associated with the processing of language, especially the processing of unfamiliar or unexpected words. Neurologists consider the N400 to be a "late" brain wave occurring four-tenths of a second after a person perceives a sound, after a good deal of neural processing has already taken place.

The test subjects focused on a dot in the center of a computer screen and listened to a long series of recorded puns. After each one, the computer screen flashed a yes-or-no statement related to that pun, which participants answered by pressing specified buttons. By analyzing the resulting N400 waves and correlating them with the visual field, either left or right, which the subjects used to read the follow-up statements, the researchers could measure whether participants "got" a pun or not, how fast they deciphered it and which parts of the brain were involved.

One representative pun that participants listened to was "College-bred is a four-year loaf made out of the old man's dough." Immediately afterward, the following statement appeared on their screen: "Parents pay for their children's tuition." If a subject answered yes it meant that he or she had recognized at least one of the puns in the original statement.

The puns used, culled from a variety of Web sites, all featured their key word at the end. Like most puns, they forced
the listener to reevaluate the intended meaning of the entire
phrase. Sample test puns included:

> The soda called his dad Pop.

> A ham walked out of a hospital and said, "I'm
> cured."

> Dermatologists make rash decisions.

> I could have been a psychiatrist, but the thought
> made me shrink.

> An archeologist's career ended in ruins.

While these puns might strike the casual listener as juvenile
or simple, they actually make complex demands on the brain.
As the researchers point out, puns require the brain to maintain multiple meanings of a word simultaneously, rather than
simply suppressing the competition or choosing an outright
winner, as it often does when confronted with ambiguity. And
while both hemispheres engage when called on to process a
pun, the left hemisphere is quicker to grasp its secondary
meanings.

Some neurologists use the term "Bayesian" to describe the
brain's capacity to wrestle with ambiguity, after the insights of
Thomas Bayes, the eighteenth-century clergyman and mathe-
matician who conceived a quantitative method for interpreting
observations. Bayes showed how to accurately estimate the

probability of various scenarios, given the level of confidence one has about the evidence presented.

Consider how simple it is to solve a "forward" problem such as 2+2=?

It's another challenge altogether to work backward by asking ?=4, because there are infinite ways to arrive at 4 via multiplication, division, addition, subtraction and combinations thereof, to mention just a few. Bayesian analysis offers a mathematical approach to working backward to identify the best solution or solutions, by asking: How many ways can one interpret this information, and why?

In another context, we witness a form of Bayesian analysis when we watch TV shows such as *Law & Order*, when detectives examine a crime scene for clues. In this case, they assign relative weight to various pieces of evidence, from the fact that a victim is dead (100 percent certainty) to the likely time of the crime (usually less than 100 percent certainty) to the potential motives and alibis of competing suspects (also highly variable). By weighting and comparing the evidence to identify inconsistencies, they eventually arrive at a conclusion and arrest the most likely perpetrator, sometimes without total certainty.

Now think of the analogous Bayesian problem in terms of language. How do we figure out a speaker's intended meaning based on an answer—either a word or words—which could have flowed logically from multiple intents and that sound very similar or exactly the same?

A distraught patient rushes into a psychologist's office. "Doctor, doctor! I think I'm a wigwam, then I think I'm a tepee. I'm a wigwam, I'm a tepee. I'm a wigwam, I'm a tepee . . ."

"Relax," the shrink says. "You're just too tense."

Upon hearing an ambiguous word (or any word, for that matter), the brain must work backward to make its best educated guess about the speaker's intent, including the possibility that this intent is to convey multiple meanings. Given the statistical certainty that every pun will seem novel to some listener, the human brain can't necessarily rely on the frequency of a word's most common use to make its best estimate. Instead, it has to qualitatively judge all available evidence to resolve the apparent incongruity.

Sometimes, such incongruity must account for lexical combinations beyond those of a single word. In an engaging book entitled *Mathematics and Humor*, Temple University Mathematics Professor John Allen Paulos offers the following examples:

Interviewer: "Do you consider clubs appropriate for small children?"

W. C. Fields: "Only when kindness fails."

Or consider this second example: "Colds can be positive or negative. Sometimes the ayes have it, and sometimes the noes."

Neither is a clean exchange. In each case, the brain confronts two *sets* of words that can have very different meanings, and not just due to phonological overlap of key words. It's the brain's ability to quickly recognize the incongruous interpretations and catch the unexpected secondary meanings that imbues them with humor.

The speed involved here is remarkable, sometimes as fast as 150 milliseconds from hearing to interpretation. Jos J. A. Van Berkum, a psycholinguist in the Netherlands, argues that when people hear a word "the brain responds to the fit between word and context well before people have actually heard the end of the word." Coincidentally, top online search engines currently attempt to mimic this ability. Even before a user has finished typing in the subject of their search, computer algorithms are already returning a provisional list of search results based on the still incomplete search request. Similar software generating predictive type on computers and mobile devices aims to save users the trouble of typing in entire words while writing or text messaging.

In much the same way, the impatient brain gets busy factoring in information to supplement basic semantic rules, including stereotyped expectations associated with the speaker's accent, in a frenzied attempt to make sense of what the person is saying before they're even done speaking. "Although we as (psycho)linguists might like things to occur in neatly ordered steps," Van Berkum writes, "the linguistic brain seems much more 'messy' and opportunistic, taking any partial cue that seems to bear on interpretation into account as soon as it can."

In essence, the brain is trying to predict what's coming next, even if it means breaking the rules of syntax and then backtracking as necessary. According to Van Berkum, the brain actually takes shortcuts, using its familiarity with what we tend to talk about to make a back-of-the-envelope analysis without waiting for all the details.

And that Bayesian eagerness to complete someone else's sentences might explain why our N400 waves spike with puns, as the surprised brain doubles back on its assumptions. With efficiency in mind, the brain apparently learns from its missteps and adjusts expectations accordingly. In a 2005 study published in the journal *Brain and Language*, a group of researchers from Harvard Medical School and other institutions ran fMRI tests on people to see if the brain actually reduces the reaction time it needs to make a judgment when a given stimulus is related to words or pictures they've just encountered.

Punsters who spar regularly with each other won't be surprised with the study's result: After priming, reaction time drops. Apparently, once you're onto a given topic, your brain's ability to associate semantically related information accelerates. So if someone says "doctor," that primes your brain to access words like *nurse, hospital, ambulance* and so on. In other words, when you're really in the groove and all those puns, good or bad, just keep coming, there's probably a neurological basis for that somewhere in the lateral and posterior superior temporal lobes. Cell by cell, the brain is unlocking meanings from sound and recombining them lickety-split. Biologically speaking, that's what makes dueling punsters so quick—they're actually priming each other's brain.

Curiously, our brains slow down for puns of a sexual nature. In a study published in the *Archives of Sexual Behavior*, researchers at Louisiana State University found that the brain processed sexual double entendres more slowly, most likely because of "editing" by listeners who automatically evaluate the social repercussions of a risqué interpretation. This delay was especially pronounced among women. According to one of the study's authors, LSU psychology professor James Geer, people have limited mental resources to apply to any given task. "If the task generates an emotion," he told *Psychology Today*, "this uses up some of those resources, and work on the task is slowed down."

This basic insight bolsters what has become a general consensus among scientists studying language: that our capacity to process words (and by extension, to pun) is based on relatively new, jury-rigged connections between several existing brain systems, rather than on a single core processor that evolved to meet that specific need. Studies have found that different people actually use different combinations of brain systems to process language, or use them to different degrees.

Such differences often show up between men and women when they're deciding if something is funny or not. In a 2004 Stanford University study published in the *Proceedings of the National Academy of Sciences*, twenty people were inserted, sequentially, into the scanning tube of a Signa 3T MRI machine, a cube-shaped apparatus almost as big as a minivan and fitted with a customized head-restraint system to prevent any movement that laughter might trigger.

The test subjects were then shown a series of cartoons, most of them captioned, which had been previously categorized as funny or not funny. When each cartoon appeared, subjects pressed a button to indicate whether they found it funny or not. Afterward, they ranked those they'd classified as funny on a 1 10 scale.

In layman's terms, the researchers found that both men and women activated common brain regions typically associated with semantic processing and the resolution of incongruity. Women, however, used some areas more, particularly in the left prefrontal cortex. This finding is consistent with evidence that women, compared to men, often have a relatively larger Broca's area, a brain region in the left prefrontal cortex associated with speech production.

In addition to these differences in processing humor, three other divergent results emerged. First, women were quicker to dismiss a cartoon as not funny. Second, women were less apt to expect a cartoon to be funny. In other words, they had lower expectations than men. Third, the dopamine rewards they experienced when a cartoon actually did seem funny were higher. However, the researchers suggest that this intensity of reward might not have been due to the fact that women found a given cartoon any funnier than the men did on an absolute scale, but rather that they had lower expectations from the outset.

But why would natural selection have produced such gender differences in the way our brains process semantic incongruity, the resolution of which lies at the heart of most humor? What competitive advantage would this offer the human species? And how does humor itself contribute to the survival of the fittest?

## EVOLUTION AND ELOCUTION

Robert Provine is a psychology professor and the assistant director of the neuroscience program at the University of Maryland–Baltimore County. He's also one of the world's experts on the science of laughter. He notes that people too often confuse humor and laughter, which can and do occur independently of each other. And from an evolutionary standpoint, Provine argues, laughter came before humor.

"Laughter is literally the ritualization of rough-and-tumble play, in which panting, ah-ah-ah, becomes ha-ha-ha," he said, adding that the first joke in human history was most likely a feigned tickle.

In his book, *Laughter: A Scientific Investigation*, Provine theorizes that laughter first became possible about six million years ago, when humans began to diverge from chimpanzees and walk upright. Bipedal locomotion offered humans many competitive advantages, not least of which was the use of two limbs for complex tasks other than walking.

But Provine suggests another advantage as well: walking

upright freed the human thorax (roughly, the area enclosed by our ribcage) from the all-consuming mechanical demands associated with four-legged locomotion. This loosened the constraints that movement-related breathing had previously placed on the use of the lungs, allowing for greater and more frequent vocalization. "To speak, or to produce any other vocalization, is to periodically override or modify our most basic need, breathing," Provine writes. "The ability to override so vital a function as breathing in the service of sound making was a revolutionary event in neurobehavioral evolution." In other words, learning to walk upright laid the physiological foundation that made language, which would not yet develop for millions of years, a feasible possibility.

Curiously, another species of four-legged land mammals overcame this same constraint between breathing and vocalization in a completely different way, by evolving into whales. Like humans, these large mammals also have extraordinary breath control and intriguing vocalization skills.

Walking upright, however, was not necessarily a step up in all regards, at least not for women. An efficient gait, one with less side-to-side motion, came at the cost of the wider hips that make birthing relatively easy for other primates. The resulting, lower human birthrate required compensatory survival skills to make up the difference. Among those that emerged, most likely about 150,000 years ago in East Africa, were the interrelated capacities for language and for abstract thinking. In essence, these skills allowed people to envision and plan for one's survival and communicate with others to achieve it. Eventually, language and abstract thinking also enabled people to develop something else that's helpful in challenging circumstances: a sense of humor.

Intuitively, we all know how useful a sense of humor can be—to entertain, to flirt, to convince, to defuse. But what is its unifying biological purpose? Why is it so common, in different forms, across cultures and time? Two researchers at the University of California at Los Angeles, Thomas Flamson and Clark Barrett, have proposed an "encryption theory" that seems to explain why. Intentional humor, they write, is akin to a lock and key. To unlock humorous content hiding beneath the surface of a joke, one needs the right key, and that key is specific but unstated common knowledge that the joke's teller and listener both share.

By broadcasting such encrypted information through a joke, a speaker can quickly assess the underlying knowledge, attitudes and inclinations of a given listener—a useful shorthand for their suitability as a collaborator, friend or mate. While still extremely helpful today, this ability to joke and bond was surely even more important in prehistoric times, when belonging to a group was critical for survival. Even in primitive forms, humor probably helped people develop the richly cooperative social structures that enabled them to survive, not just emotionally but physically. Essentially, if you got the joke, you got into the cave and then into the sack, and hopefully into the gene pool of the next generation.

Over eons, this capacity for humor became more and more hardwired. Properly stimulated with the right joke, quip or pun—all of which are encrypted abstractions—the brain's reward centers eventually came to generate actual, physical signals of pleasure, which in turn reinforced the social benefits of sharing humor. Over time, as intellectual capacities rose in relative importance in the competition for mates, those with better verbal skills and a stronger sense of humor probably started getting the last laugh more and more often. Around the camp-fire, he who regularly laid an egg, didn't.

Modern medical studies suggest that experiencing humor may yield a wide range of health benefits: reducing stress, enhancing cardiovascular fitness, and boosting the immune and endocrine systems —all of which help in overcoming the challenges of survival and reproduction. So as we rose from all fours, it seems that we all became stand-up comedians, or died trying. Given this gradual evolution, it's highly probable that the first time a *Homo sapien* deliberately made a pun was probably long before any listener understood it as funny, caved in, and laughed. Even in prehistoric humor, timing was everything.

Today most humor, especially semantic humor, remains an ephemeral, subjective experience. Three people who speak the same language can hear the same sentence containing a pun and their brains might parse the sounds and process them entirely differently. "Did you hear about Robin Hood? He just had an arrow escape." One person might hear the pun ("an arrow escape" v. "a narrow escape") and, given the legendary bandit's frequent encounters with the Sheriff of Nottingham, find it cleverly amusing. Another might hear the pun and shrug with indifference. A third might miss the pun altogether. In each case, it all comes down to how a person's brain perceives and resolves ambiguity.

Scientists believe that this complex task—resolving ambiguous, often incongruous information—underpins the brain's perception of humor. Instinctively, all people seek to establish a coherent narrative to explain what they see and hear. It's how we make sense of the world. We experience humor when, under certain circumstances, the temporal-occipital junction (above the ear on both sides) detects unexpected, ambiguous incongruity, and other areas (including Broca's area, near our left temple) scramble to revise the initial storyline to reestablish coherence.

Perhaps more than any other type of humor, homophonic puns both drive and depend on this ambiguity. For a split second, they manage to hold open the elevator doors of language and meaning as the brain toggles furiously between competing semantic destinations, before finally deciding which is the best answer—or deciding to live with both.

Research suggests that "getting" a pun is a two-step process. Consider the following riddle, which researchers posed, among other semantic jokes and puns, to subjects in a 2001 fMRI study seeking to identify how the brain processes semantic jokes:

"Why did the golfer wear two sets of pants?"

"He got a hole in one."

Encountering this joke, our brain instantly engages its posterior temporal lobe, which strives to resolve the ambiguity— torn pants, or a good shot—by juxtaposing possible semantic answers and evaluating their relative merits. If our brain fails to sort out the ambiguity, the pun fails. Alternatively, if our brain identifies the correct answer (or answers) and resolves the initial ambiguity, other parts of the brain, including the medial ventral prefrontal cortex, kick in to evaluate it for its degree of "funniness."

Not surprisingly, some people find the pun funny, and some don't. This difference doesn't just show up on their faces, it shows up in distinct patterns of brain activity, because we actually use different neural pathways to process puns than we do for other types of jokes.

Given that there are so many variables at play, it's not yet possible to fully untangle the pun's path through the brain. Yes, modern imaging technology lets us see all those neurons raising a ruckus. But for all that sound and fury, experts can't yet offer us a detailed picture of how it all works.

# CHAPTER 3

# *To Pun or Not to Pun:*
# *The Risible Fall of Puns*
# *Through Time*

SOME YEARS AGO, A GREEK IMMIGRANT LIVING ON NEW YORK'S
Lower East Side rushed into a tailor's shop with a pair of torn
black trousers. The old tailor, seated behind his sewing machine, slowly put on a pair of wire-rimmed spectacles and began to examine the threadbare garment, stitch by stitch.

Impatient, the customer began to tap his foot. The tailor, not
one to be rushed, continued his careful examination. After
what seemed an eternity, he looked up with a question.
"Euripides?"

The customer snapped, "Eumenides?"

For most people who like puns and catch the reference to Greek drama, the exchange is funny—at least the first time. For others, such humor just seems to needle. Because when it comes to puns, many people consider all of them—no matter how clever—to be foolish, irritating, subversive or worse.

"A pun is *primâ facie* an insult to the person you are talking with. It implies utter indifference to or sublime contempt for his remarks, no matter how serious," wrote the nineteenth-century physician, poet and humorist Oliver Wendell Holmes, Sr. "People who make puns are like wanton boys that put coppers on the railroad tracks. They amuse themselves and other children, but their little trick may upset a freight train of conversation for the sake of a battered witticism."

In his 1848 book *The Autocrat of the Breakfast Table*, Holmes took an even tougher stance. He wrote that "a pun does not commonly justify a blow in return. But if a blow were given for such cause, and death ensued, the jury would be judges of both the facts and of the pun, and might, if the latter were of an aggravated character, return a verdict of justifiable homicide." Perhaps incorrigible punsters should be grateful that it wasn't Holmes, but rather his eponymous son, who became a Supreme Court justice.

Another critic of the pun was William Shawn, longtime editor of *The New Yorker*. As Daniel Menaker recounts in his book *A Good Talk*, Shawn was editing a first-person article Menaker had written about hitchhiking through Manhattan during a transit strike. The piece, slated for the magazine's Talk of the Town section, closed with the following exchange between Menaker and another pedestrian: "I asked him how he was getting around, and he said, 'Diesel.' I said, 'Diesel?' He pointed to his feet and said, 'Diesel get me anywhere.'"

Shawn cut the entire exchange. Just before the piece was going to press, Menaker tried to slip it back in. Shawn caught wind of the change and promptly summoned the writer to his office.

"Mr. Menaker, I understand you want to put back the original ending of your 'Talk' story," he said.

"I know we usually don't use puns, but this one seemed pretty good," Menaker answered.

Shawn "smiled in pain" and put an end to the argument, declaring: "I think you must not understand that to use this pun would *destroy the magazine*."

Holmes (the elder) and Shawn are not alone in their loathing of puns. Many other prominent writers and thinkers have similarly decried them as cheap, weeds, cowpats, the lowest form of humor, pitiable imbecility and "the most groveling kind of wit."

"If we must lash one another, let it be with the manly strokes of wit and satire," wrote Joseph Addison, a fierce critic of the form, in 1711. "For I am of the old philosopher's opinion, that if I must suffer from one or the other, I would rather it should be from the paw of the lion than from the hoof of an ass."

To many people, such antipathy is no surprise. Because just as most of us know a few people who can't resist making puns, we also know others who can't stand them no matter what. Historically speaking, however, such antipathy and its cloak of intellectual respectability constitute a relatively new development in Western civilization. In fact, for thousands of years, the pun actually enjoyed a privileged status in Western philosophy, art and religion—a status that far transcended that which it often suffers today.

So what happened? How did the pun, especially the English

pun, fall so far from grace? Its decline, as it turns out, was caused by the combined and prolonged influence of several interrelated forces—political, cultural and technological—on the English language generally, and on puns specifically. To understand these, we need to step back a thousand years and trace a few entwined threads that weave their way throughout the tapestry of English history.

## OF NORMS, AND NORMANS

On a blustery October morning in 1066, a bloody, exhausted line of English soldiers hurried into position atop a low ridgeline in Sussex, standing shoulder to shoulder to form a makeshift wall of battered shields. Gripping their battle-axes, they watched as a vast army, perhaps as many as ten thousand French soldiers, assembled for attack.

For the English, it had been a long, forced march—hundreds of miles in a handful of days—to meet these fresh invaders. But what other choice did they have? Still recovering from their hard-fought victory against Norwegian invaders to the north, this southern threat was graver still. William, Duke of Normandy, had laid claim to the English throne and seemed determined to seize it.

The English king, Harold Godwinson, was in no mood to surrender. A tall, articulate warrior-king, he was no stranger to battle and rallied his troops with speech and sword alike. He had just led them to a decisive victory at Stamford Bridge, and God willing, he would do so here, too. And so, with their boots soaked, their chain mail heavy and their wounds still oozing blood through dirty bandages, his soldiers steeled themselves for the downpour that was about to fall—not of rain, but of arrows.

On William's command, some eight hundred French archers let their arrows fly, a thicket of darts humming through the air. As that first volley thudded into the English shields, Harold's men roared with righteous, prideful anger. But in the hours of bloody battle that followed—axe against shield, spear against sword, lance against pitchfork—the English struggled to hold the line. Sometime after midday, William had his archers start aiming higher, over the shields, sowing havoc behind the wavering, gap-toothed wall. And as those arrows fell, so, too, did King Harold, a feathered shaft through his right eye.

This was no mere *flèche* wound; it pierced the ebbing English hopes for good. With Harold dead, the rout was on, and by nightfall the Battle of Hastings was over. While it would take another two months for William to bring the last of the English nobles into submission, his invasion was a fait accompli. On Christmas Day, under the soaring stone vaults of Westminster Abbey, William the Conqueror was crowned King of England.

William spoke French, not English, and his victory would have a profound impact on the English language. At that time, English was a mixture of Old German, Norse, Latin, Gaelic, Pictish, Welsh and perhaps the echoes of Celtic grammar. As such, it bore little resemblance to the language we speak today. It had verbs of ten types, nouns of three genders, and a complexity of endings that would boggle the most astute of today's grammarians.

As king, William swiftly imposed French as the language of the royal bureaucracy, and replaced both the English nobility and its clergy with ambitious arrivistes from France. Naturally, these Frenchmen conducted their business—from parliament to the courts to the church—in their native tongue. In official matters, both written and spoken, English was history—so much so that for more than three centuries after the Norman invasion, no king of England spoke English as his first language.

Which is not to say that English disappeared. Far from it. Because even as the Norman elite parlayed their victory into economic and ecclesiastical authority, the vast majority of English people continued speaking their mother tongue. Inevitably, the two languages began to influence each other. Over time, English absorbed an estimated ten thousand French words, including *debonair*, *décolletage* and, notably, *double entendre*. Meanwhile, as Normans began to intermarry with English-speakers and have children, these successive generations were often bilingual, until eventually French (and French identity) fell away in England altogether.

Apart from enriching English with a wealth of descriptive vocabulary, the imposition of French as England's official language had another beneficial effect. Because English in this period was mostly spoken, not written, it was able to evolve more quickly (as all languages do over time) unrestrained by the shackles of "official" grammar. So by the fourteenth century, when English began to reemerge as a written language, people had dramatically simplified its grammar and spelling. And while quite a few remnants of its contributory languages survived (*knot*, *haggle* and *law,* for example, are of Norse origin), a modern hybrid, what historian John McWhorter calls "our magnificent bastard tongue," was beginning to put down its roots.

## OF PARASITES, PLAYWRIGHTS AND PUNS

In 1348, however, another wave of invaders scrambled down the mooring lines of arriving merchant ships, this time at Weymouth. Nobody saw them coming, but who could, really? Hitching a ride in the warm fur of Asian rats, the common flea, each the size of a pinhead, drew little blood compared to the arrows of William the Conqueror. But these particular fleas, infected with bacteria causing bubonic plague, were far more prolific and much more deadly.

Among humans, a single bite from an infected flea often triggered a raging fever, vomiting, and the eruption of oozing boils around the neck, armpits and groin. Two of three infected people would be dead within days, their corpses often left to rot as those able to flee the mysterious onslaught sought escape in the next village, only to fan fear and outbreak alike.

The resulting pandemic, known as the Black Death, killed off a third of Europe's population in just fifty years, including more than a million people in England alone. Soon, entire English estates were devoid of agricultural workers. Children were left orphans. Churchmen, including many of the country's remaining French speakers, died by the drove or abandoned their monastaries altogether. Thriving hamlets became ghost towns almost overnight. The resulting social and economic disruption was severe, breaking down class structure and driving mass migrations. From a linguistic standpoint, this massive social upheaval stirred together people with strongly distinct regional accents and, in a world turned upside down, change became the norm.

As a consequence, London became a teeming boomtown in the fifteenth and sixteenth centuries, flooded by tens of thousands of newcomers speaking a wide range of languages and dialects.

As the rest of Europe, too, recovered from the plague and sea trade grew, sailors and merchants brought back thousands of new loan words from the Continent, Africa and Asia. Meanwhile, a renewed interest in classical literature, both Greek and Roman, introduced even more new vocabulary into English, along with a taste for modern Italian. Amid all this linguistic tumult, spelling was largely a personal choice, assuming one could read and write.

From the 1500s onward, however, this swirling amalgamation of foreign words, spellings and pronunciations drew sharp criticism from conservatives (much like modern proponents of "English Only" standards in the United States currently decry the use of immigrant languages). It was Sir John Cheke, a scholar whom Henry VIII appointed as the first Regius Professor of Greek at Cambridge University, who led the charge. "I am of this opinion that our own tung shold be written cleane and pure, unmixt and unmangeled with borrowing of other tunges," Cheke wrote. The tide of change, however, proved unstoppable.

By any measure, English was a rapidly changing, freewheeling language with an unprecedented wealth of homophones—words that sound the same but have different meanings. All these homophones provided endless raw material for punsters of every station.

"Clergymen punned in the pulpit, judges upon the bench, statesmen at the council-board, and even criminals in their dying speeches," one scholar of the period wrote. When Sir Francis Drake, the dashing privateer, navigator and vice admiral helped defeat the Spanish Armada in 1588, he purportedly dispatched a messenger to Queen Elizabeth (who spoke six languages) bearing a one-word pun in Latin: *cantharides*—the name of an aphrodisiac better known as "the Spanish fly."

Playwrights of the era including William Shakespeare, Christopher Marlowe and Ben Jonson also punned with abandon, sometimes even making up new words to suit their needs. Because English, long denigrated as a lowly vernacular in comparison to the more ecclesiastical Latin or Greek, suddenly seemed to offer endless possibilities for play, such wordplay quickly became, according to Shakespeare scholar Hëlge Kökeritz, "as much a part of sophisticated conversation as it was a stock ingredient of contemporary comedy."

"Shakespeare's penchant for punning," Kökeritz wrote, "reflects the spirit of the age." Not that Shakespeare was an average punster by any measure. He was far and away the best of his era and used puns to reveal not just his own wit but the knowledge and depth of the characters who uttered them.

Fundamentally though, Shakespeare and his fellow playwrights punned because puns helped engage and entertain audiences, many of which included illiterate but clever tradespeople whose ears were highly attuned to jokes, innuendos and double meanings. It enticed them to pay close attention to the speaker's intent or miss the moment, which was vitally important in an age of live performance. At capacity, the thatched galleries of London's Globe Theater held about 3,000 people, and the most popular plays could quickly make a big impression in a city of only 200,000.

While plays were popular entertainment, though, they often conveyed not-so-subtle political or social commentary, too. "To an Elizabethan the play upon words was not merely an elegance of style and a display of wit; it was also a means of emphasis and an instrument of persuasion," wrote Frank Wilson, author of *Shakespeare and the Diction of Common Life*. "An argument might be conducted from step to step—and in the pamphleteers it often is—by a series of puns. The genius of the language encouraged them."

With this in mind, dramatists used puns for yet another reason: to outwit censorship imposed by the monarch's "Master of the Revels." Consider the cobbler in the opening scene of Shakespeare's *Julius Caesar*. "Truly, sir, all that I live by is with the awl," the cobbler says. "I meddle with no tradesman's matters, nor women's matters, but withal I am, indeed, sir, a surgeon to old shoes." It all sounds innocent enough, but as Frankie Rubinstein notes in *A Dictionary of Shakespeare's Sexual Puns and Their Significance*, audiences of the time would have caught what were then obvious double entendres about using a phallic tool to play doctor with "old shoes," meaning prostitutes.

Such puns managed to slip past Queen Elizabeth's Master of the Revels, just as they would frustrate, several centuries later, the Shakespeare scholar (and father of the modern dictionary) Samuel Johnson. Today some of Shakespeare's wordplay, especially rhymes and rhyming puns, can sound a little awkward, or even forced. But that's largely because the pronunciation of certain words has evolved, breaking apart couples that once danced together gracefully. With this in mind, Kökeritz, a noted scholar of archaic English pronunciation, has suggested that perhaps as many as half of Shakespeare's homophonic puns have been lost in the modern era.

It's also important to note that many of Shakespeare's puns, including most in his tragedies, weren't even intended to be funny in the first place. In the second act of *Macbeth*, Lady Macbeth describes how she will incriminate the innocent by smearing them—gilding them—with the king's blood.

"If he doe bleed,
Ile guild the faces of the Groomes withall,
For it must seeme their Guilt."

While the archaic spelling might initially confuse modern readers, guilt—that is, culpability—sounds identical to gilt, as in the layering on of gold or, in this case, blood. The pun is clearly clever, yet anything but funny. One should remember, though, that puns are at their core defined by multiplicity of meaning, not necessarily humor. The common expectation that puns should always be funny, or die in the attempt, is a relatively modern development.

When *Macbeth* was first performed, most likely in 1611, the pun was a common rhetorical device for both comic and dramatic purposes. Poets, playwrights and preachers alike used it often as a tool to prise open the full meaning of language, and thereby more fully express the human experience.

Even a serious Elizabethan poet such as John Donne, who penned a great deal of deeply meditative religious poetry, punned to make his point. Sometime around 1622, struggling to recover from a serious illness, Donne (which rhymes with "sun") wrote "A Hymn to God the Father," playing on his own name to beg forgiveness from his creator. By the end of the first verse, he is already punning.

"When Thou hast done, Thou hast not done, For I have more." According to historical accounts, the poem was put to music and sung under the great dome of St. Paul's Cathedral, in London.

Donne, Shakespeare and their contemporaries were all influenced, to a significant degree, by the Renaissance and its associated embrace of all things classical. This included the art of rhetoric and its use of puns, a respectable tradition that could be traced back to Homer's epics and beyond.

In ancient Athens, Plato himself punned, and Aristotle expounded upon such metaphorical wordplay in his instructional treatise, *Rhetoric*. In the book, which is still in print, Aristotle both highlights and praises the use of clever, well-constructed semantic surprises to introduce a new idea or establish a new connection. "In all these jokes, whether a word is used in a second sense or metaphorically, the joke is good if it fits the facts," he wrote. "Well-constructed riddles are attractive for the same reason."

Roman orators later put an even greater emphasis on such wordplay, as recorded by Cicero in his classic series *De Oratore*. "Wit and humor are always very agreeable, and often highly serviceable," Cicero wrote. "Equivocal sayings are esteemed as being of the wittiest kind, but they are not always employed in jests, they are sometimes applied seriously."

All across Renaissance Europe, not just in England, people were giving this rich, ancient tradition a fresh voice. In 1528, a dashing soldier and Papal diplomat named Baldesar Castiglione published his *Book of the Courtier*, a handbook of sorts for proper behavior in the courts of nobility. The topic of punning, specifically how to pun in good taste, merited an entire section.

Conceding that puns "are more usually praised for their ingenuity than for their humor," Castiglione urged speakers to "be cautious in their use, hunting carefully for the right words, and avoiding those that cause the joke to fall flat and seem too laboured, or, as we have said, that are too wounding."

Punning was similarly popular among Europe's court jesters, whom in earlier times had been known as bards, minstrels, troubadours or fools. In an age when travel was still difficult and dangerous, those who did were automatically suspect. Traveling entertainers, especially, were commonly viewed as vagabonds, tricksters or parasites. Jesters, even those who stayed put, suffered a similar reputation. So while keeping a court jester was something of a status symbol among Europe's nobility, the jesters themselves were often of low status.

Many of those employed by royal courts were people who suffered a severe physical deformity, such as dwarfism. As such, they lived entirely by their wits and talent for entertainment, totally dependent on their patrons for food, shelter and protection. They entertained well—punning, riddling, singing, making music, or juggling—or paid for their failure with physical abuse such as dunkings, beatings, or being tossed up and down in a blanket. Sometimes, such inhumane abuse *was* the entertainment. As such, juggling double meanings and dishing out thinly disguised satire were often a jester's only hope of escape, or recourse.

Given their direct access to royalty, however, a few of these court insiders also managed to acquire wealth, and even political influence as they voiced "crazy" opinions that ordinary courtiers would never dare utter. One such joker was Archy Armstrong, jester to England's Charles I. Like many of his brethren, Armstrong was a dwarf. Born poor, somewhere near the Scottish border, he got his start stealing sheep but eventually found his way, as a jester, into the royal household. In return for his loyal service, Armstrong was eventually rewarded with a pension, a monopoly on the burgeoning trade in tobacco pipes, and an estate of one thousand acres in Ireland.

But as his stature continued to grow in the palace, "King Archy," as he became known, acquired enemies. First among them was the Archbishop of Canterbury, William Laud, who vied for influence with the king and couldn't stand his irreverent rival. In one famous instance, the king, the archbishop and Armstrong were about to dine at the Palace of Whitehall, and the king asked Armstrong, not the man who crowned him, to say grace. With a smirk, Armstrong drove the knife in with a perfectly unassailable pun: "Great praise be given to God and little *laud* to the Devil."

It took a few years, but the incensed archbishop eventually got the last laugh. In 1637, he finally persuaded the king to oust Armstrong and had the royal privy council sentence the jester "to have his coat pulled over his head and be discharged [from] the king's service and banished from the king's court." Angry but ever adaptable to change, Armstrong launched a new career as a moneylender.

## TORTURED ENGLISH

Though Laud had finally managed to silence the irreverent punster, his troubles were really just beginning, as he and the royal family struggled to stave off the growing political power of a group of zealous religious conservatives known as Puritans. One of their leaders was William Prynne, a Puritan lawyer who in 1632 published *Histriomastix*, a thousand-page diatribe against the monarchy and society's moral corruption. Laud had Prynne locked up in the Tower of London and tried for seditious libel, on the grounds that he used "implicite meanes" to suggest the legality of overthrowing the monarchy. Convicted, he was pilloried and had the tops of his ears snipped off.

Undeterred, Prynne continued to publish anonymous pamphlets, even when he was arrested and imprisoned again. One such pamphlet, which urged church wardens to defy their bishops, featured an elaborate initial letter *C* in the style of an illuminated manuscript. It was an unlikely flourish from a Puritan known for aesthetic restraint. But when tipped on its side, the C looked just like the pope's head, faced by an army of soldiers and ordinary men. Prynne's letter was a visual pun.

The Holy See was none too pleased. Nor was King Charles (married to a Catholic), and especially not the apoplectic Laud. On discovering the identity of the pamphlet's author, Laud had Prynne hauled before the Star Chamber yet again. Convicted once more of seditious libel, he was sentenced this time to public branding, and his cheeks were burned with an *S* and an *L*. According to one account, the sentence was carried out to the very letter of the law: when the hangman "burnte one cheeke with a letter the wrong waye," he promptly rebranded Prynne's face to correct his typographical error.

Rumors swept London that Prynne had died from the punishment, but it was too early to print this rebel's epitaph. Even before his guards had bundled him back into the Tower, he was busy composing a blistering, punning verse of defiance. Half English, half Latin, it played off of the double meaning of *Stigmata Laudis*—the glorious stigmata, akin to the wounds that Christ himself suffered upon the cross, only this time inflicted by Laud. Ironically, far from branding Prynne with shame, Laud had transformed the incorrigible punster into a political and religious martyr.

If Prynne was stoic, though, others were unwilling to turn the other cheek. Popular opposition to the church and monarchy continued to escalate. In 1641, desperate to regain control of the increasingly bitter public debate, King Charles led four hundred soldiers to Westminster to arrest his principal parliamentary critics. His targets escaped, and the gambit only threw fuel onto the fire of his opponents.

Within days the king was forced to flee London. Within months, England was engulfed in a bloody civil war. For Prynne, that meant vindication and release from prison. For Laud, it spelled the beginning of the end, and he was soon behind bars himself. Finally, after a show trial in which Prynne played chief prosecutor, Laud found himself kneeling in prayer one last time, his head atop the chopping block.

The ensuing years were rough for England. While Parliamentary forces (in alliance with the Puritans) quickly prevailed in most areas, King Charles and his Royalists held out elsewhere, until finally forced to take refuge in Scotland. In 1649, the Scots handed over the deposed king to the Parliamentary forces. After a short trial for treason, he was led to a scaffold in front of the very palace he had once called home, and was beheaded with a single stroke of the axe.

Within a few years, England was under the iron rule of a grim and puritanical general, Oliver Cromwell. As England's Lord Protector, Cromwell imposed a series of increasingly draconian measures of social and religious control throughout England. Among other things, he imposed strict censorship, banned all plays, established a female dress code, suspended most sporting events, tore down the famous Globe Theatre, nixed the traditional celebration of Christmas and even outlawed pie—those who dared bake them did so charily.

Mercifully, Cromwell died in 1658, and England's totalitarian religious fever began to break. By 1661, the religious zealots were marginalized and a more independent and moderate parliament began liberalizing the country once again. They relaxed censorship, reopened the theaters, loosened up social controls and even restored a limited monarchy, with a second King Charles atop the throne.

The pun, like a pinecone that survives a forest fire, was soon sprouting anew. As the story goes, when the king was told that his jester, the playwright Charles Killigrew, could pun on any subject, he issued a challenge and commanded that Killigrew "make one on me."

Instantly, Killigrew quipped that this was impossible, because "the king is no subject."

It was a clever retort, even if the king was actually somewhat constrained by an assertive, postwar parliament. Yet, if the Restoration was a good time to be king, relatively speaking, it was an even better time for English punsters, many of whom began to fill London's burgeoning coffeehouses.

## GROUNDS FOR DISPUTE

The city's first coffeehouse had opened in 1652, perhaps in response to the Puritan crackdown on public drunkenness, in a shed behind a church in the central Cornhill neighborhood. Right away, it drew a devoted clientele. Only a decade later, there were eighty-two such establishments in the city, and they were already sparking complaints from competing tavern keepers and also authorities, who feared the freewheeling, sometimes subversive discourse the coffeehouses seemed to inspire.

Neither were entirely wrong to feel threatened. Right from the start, coffeehouses had taken off as popular social hubs where people of different classes (and in a few documented

cases, sexes) began to mix and exchange commercial news, political opinion, literary manuscripts, scientific ideas, palace gossip and humor, including puns.

One 1662 anonymous satire was entitled, in part, *The Tryall
of the Coffee-Man: Wherein He Is Indicted, Arraigned, Convicted,
and Condemned, by Sir Benjamin Bacchus, Sir Mathew Malt, Sir
Henry Hop, Sir Francis Froth, judges of the court.* The indicted
coffeeman, one Don Ballingo Blackburnt, is found guilty of
stealing business from the taverns and robbing the city's men of
their virility. His sentence included, among other punishments,
immersion in coffee, a beating with bulls' penises and stoning
with sheep's testicles—a true and bitter testament to the hard
justice of the day, or at least the satirist's imagination.

Some of the punning was more overtly political. A tavern
keeper named William Hicks, writing under the pen name of
Roger L'Estrange, published a joke book in 1677 entitled *Coffee
House Jests.* In it, he recounts the punning anecdote about an
Army chaplain during the recent troubles, who had prayed
aloud asking that God bless the parliament and "grant they
may all hang together."

"Yes sir with all my heart," a bystander answered the chaplain, "and the sooner the better."

King Charles and other conservatives took a dim view of
such critiques, whether couched in humor or not. But ultimately, there wasn't a lot the king could do; his royal proclama-
tion forbidding coffeehouses from selling "coffee, chocolet,
sherbet or tea" had promised severe penalties for those who dis-
obeyed. Stirred to outrage, the city's coffeehouse owners and
their influential, caffeinated patrons had launched a furious
and popular counterattack. The king, taken aback by the brewing rebellion, had quickly capitulated.

Over the course of the next century, before tea claimed the cup as the quintessential English beverage, thousands of coffeehouses sprang up in London and throughout Britain. Many such establishments became known for specific topics of discussion and the business conducted there. One was called London's, just off Fleet Street, where publishers gathered to sell copyrights. Lloyd's became the place for maritime news and shipping insurance. The Grecian (site of the dueling scholars) often drew Fellows of the Royal Society, who gathered to discuss the latest scientific ideas. First among these coffeehouses for a time, though, was Will's Coffee-House, famous for attracting the nation's literary intelligentsia. Located just east of Covent Garden, it was nicknamed the "Wits' Coffee-House" for the quality of its witty repartee.

Among its customers were the anti-Puritan playwright William Wycherley (whose play *The Country Wife* puns unabashedly on sex), Addison (the pun critic), the poet Alexander Pope, the diarist Samuel Pepys and the revered poet and playwright John Dryden. Dryden, who held court by the fireplace during winter and on the balcony during summer, liked to call these tables his winter and his summer seat.

Dryden had a conflicted relationship with puns; while he used them liberally in his plays, he publicly disdained them. Predictably, such inconsistency drew the jibes of unapologetic punsters. In one instance, he was at the coffeehouse with his back to Poet Laureate Nicholas Rowe, when an observant punster quipped: "You are like a waterman; you look one way, and Rowe another." Dryden got angry, but the punster was right; he couldn't have it both ways—it was either or.

The writer Jonathan Swift also frequented Will's. Unlike Dryden, Swift punned without reserve or remorse, reveling in the infinite, often stinging, possibilities of language. While at this time Swift's most popular masterpiece, *Gulliver's Travels*, was still just a Lilliputian spark of an idea in the back of his mind, he was already a renowned satirist who churned out essays, poetry, pamphlets and political commentary—some high and some low.

According to Carole Fabricant, Professor of English at the University of California at Riverside, Swift, like many writers before him, exhibited a conservative impulse to stabilize the English language. But at the same time, this impulse never prevented him from bending language to suit his own needs. He often invented new words and played word games with his fellow London wits, many of them punsters-in-arms from his native Ireland.

For example, Swift, a clergyman well educated in the classics, once wrote the following nonsensical Latin verse, which might seem familiar to a generation of grammar school students:

> Mollis abuti,
> Has an acuti,
> No lasso finis,
> Molli divinis.
> Omi de armis tres,
> Imi na dist res,
> Cantu disco ver
> Meas alo ver?

Now read it phonetically:

> Moll is a beauty
> Has an acute eye,
> No lass so fine is,
> Molly divine is.

O my dear mistress,
I'm in a distress,
Can't you discover
Me as a lover?

Despite his remarkable skills and success, Swift was always something of a literary outsider, perhaps because of his Irish roots or blunt opinions. And eventually, he grew weary of the constant, caffeinated commentary at the Wit's Coffee-House and penned a short critique of the daily, literary gossip that people passed off as insight:

"Be sure at Will's the following day,
Lie snug, and hear what critics say."

Swift's pen was on the mark. In the late 1600s and early 1700s, there was no shortage of critics debating the nature of snug lies—and truth—in every possible form, and not just at Will's. From biology to physics to politics to language, provocative thinkers began to investigate, argue and discover a world of rationality. Shaking off the shackles of faith, myth and custom that had defined so much since antiquity, they sought to examine everything around them through the lens of reason.

Among other issues, puns themselves became a source of contention, a litmus test of one's views on language, meaning, and the possibility of defining absolute truth. In this Age of Enlightenment, the roots of rationalism were quickly taking over the intellectual garden, and language was no exception. As such, many came to view the pun's very ambiguity as a serious flaw. Yes, it had once been a commonly accepted rhetorical tool, but now many rationalists began dismissing it as a relic, an outdated stylistic device of ancient philosophers, aging clergy and dead playwrights.

Not that Aristotle, Cicero and other ancients had nothing worthwhile to offer, but much of their wisdom was now seen as static or outdated. By contrast, observation and experimentation provided a new, direct and more reliable way to acquire knowledge.

Compared to things, words were slippery. According to the late Washington University scholar Richard Jones, ambitious and influential scientists of the Royal Society—inspired by Sir Francis Bacon's novel and rigorous approach to scientific inquiry—were determined "to sweep away all the fogginess of words." They aimed, he wrote, "to reduce language to its simplest terms, to make it as accurate, concrete and clear an image of the material world as was possible."

"More than any other linguistic defect, scientists objected to a word's possessing many meanings or the same meaning as another word," Jones wrote. Physician and philosopher John Locke suggested that the study of mathematics helped free the mind "from the cheat of words." If the laws of nature could be reduced to mathematical formulas of unambiguous meaning, why not language? By this calculus, puns, subjective and imprecise, failed the test of rationality.

The rise of scientific thought also undermined the primacy of the Bible, whose original Hebrew texts were rich with puns. Not only did many seventeenth-century thinkers begin to question the authority of the Hebrew alphabet as God's original creation, they also began to question the utility of language, especially religious language, as a tool to describe and understand the world with any accuracy.

"The pun was just one high-profile victim of these shifts in beliefs," writes Simon Alderson, a scholar who has studied puns and punsters of the period. As attitudes toward language evolved, so did attitudes toward the language of humor, including puns. According to Alderson, "this hierarchy was adjusted in a way that tended to reflect the priorities of the New Science with its empiricist search for truth in *things* rather than *words*."

Meanwhile, advancing technology, specifically printing, also began to spell the pun's decline in social status. The first printing press in England had arrived in 1476. Over the ensuing two centuries, the spread of more presses had driven a dramatic increase in literacy. By 1600, about half of England's urban population could read and write, and the percentage only continued to rise. Printing, by its very nature, placed more binding demands on language. Surely and steadily, it helped transform what had been an oral culture into a written one and forced writers, punsters included, to commit to a single spelling before the type was set.

As printing became more accessible and affordable, both advocates and detractors of the pun used this technology to press their case in increasingly heated essays, pamphlets and satires. In 1709, Anthony Ashley-Cooper, Third Earl of Shaftesbury, took a jab at puns in his *Characteristicks of Men, Manners, Opinions, Times*. "We have seen in our own time the Decline and Ruin of a false sort of Wit, which so much delighted our Ancestors, that their Poems and Plays, as well as Sermons, were full of it," he wrote. "The very Language of the Court was Punning. But 'tis now banish'd the Town, and all good Company: There are only some few Footsteps of it in the Country; and it seems at last confin'd to the Nurserys of Youth, as the chief Entertainment of Pedants and their Pupils."

Shaftesbury, perhaps, might have felt some personal animus. Not too many years earlier, political opponents had publicly ridiculed his favorite coffeehouse, The Amsterdam, as well as his political views, in a punning broadside entitled *The Amster-damnable Coffee-House*.

Other detractors of the pun soon joined the fray. In 1711, Joseph Addison and Richard Steele launched *The Spectator*, a daily publication that Addison intended "to enliven Morality with Wit, and to temper Wit with Morality . . . till I have recovered [readers] out of that desperate State of Vice and Folly, into which the Age is fallen." Aimed primarily at the emerging middle class now patronizing the coffeehouses of London, *The Spectator* attempted to impart a sense of culture, manners and refinement.

Punning became an early target. Briefly noting punning's rise and fall from ancient times, Addison conceded that the Greeks and Romans were certainly brilliant writers and philosophers. But they also suffered, in some areas of thought, a lack of rational judgment. "The moderns cannot reach their beauties," he wrote, "but can avoid their imperfections." The pun, he asserted, had finally been "entirely banished out of the learned world."

Addison was overstating his case, and his fellow anti-punsters conceded as much, at least tacitly, by virtue of their vigorous public debate on the matter. In an anonymous 1714 satirical pamphlet entitled *God's Revenge Against Punning, Shewing the Miserable Fates of Persons Addicted to This Crying Sin, in Court and Town*, one writer drew comparisons between punning, the Black Death and the Great Fire of London, which had destroyed much of the city a half century earlier. He identified "the woeful practice of punning" as "a contagion" that had "first crept in among the first quality, descended to their footmen and infused itself into their ladies."

"This does occasion the corruption of our language, and therein the word of God translated into our language, which certainly every sober Christian must tremble at."

As evidence of God's wrath, the writer went on to cite instances of well-known punsters who were disfigured, crippled, lost the capacity to speak, broke their necks, squandered their fortune to gambling or became "great drunkards and Tories." Despite such antipathy toward puns, the pamphlet's author (probably Alexander Pope) somehow couldn't resist slipping in at least one of his own, writing that even Daniel Button, the proprietor of Will's Coffee-House was lately "deprived of his wits."

## A SWIFT RESPONSE

Unwilling to let such provocation pass, England's top punsters fired back. Among them was Swift, who in 1716 published (also anonymously) *A Modest Defence of Punning: or a compleat Answer to a scandalous and malicious Paper called God's Revenge Against Punning*. Contrary to its title, the essay was anything but modest. Rather, it was absurd, mocking and brilliant at once, interweaving pun after pun in Latin, Greek, English and French—running intellectual circles, in effect, around the anti-punsters.

Swift argued that the author of *God's Revenge Against Punning* "seems to have *founded* his whole Discourse upon one grand Mistake: And therefore his whole Discourse will be *founddead* as soon as I have removed that Mistake; which is, that He condemns the whole Art in generall [sic] without dis-

tinguishing Puns into Good and Bad: whereby it appears how
ignorant he is in Antiquity. The antient [sic] Romans very well
understood the Difference between the *fine* or *pretty* Pun, and
the *bad* Pun. . . ."

Building his argument with pun after pun, Swift even
alluded—with a rhetorical wink—to the incident some years
earlier with Rowe and Dryden, back at the Wit's Coffee-House,
"of which our Author is as ignorant as a certain Gentleman
who, reading of a *Roman Scholar*, thought *Roman* was a *Waterman* and *Scholar* a *Sculler*." To the intensely competitive Swift,
it seems, the old exchange was still *au courant*.

In 1719, Thomas Sheridan, most likely with input from
Swift, followed up with another defense of punning by publishing (pseudonymously) a booklet entitled *Ars Punica, Sive
Flos Linguarum. The Art Of Punning; Or, The Flower Of Languages: In Seventy-Nine Rules; For The Further Improvement Of
Conversation, And Help Of Memory. By The Labour And Industry Of Tom Pun-Sibi.*

*Ars Punica* asserted that "Punning, of all arts and sciences, is
the most extraordinary: for all others are circumscribed by certain bounds; but this alone is found to have no limits, because,
to excel therein requires a more extensive knowledge of all
things. A punner must be a man of the greatest natural abilities, and of the best accomplishments: his wit must be poignant
and fruitful, his understanding clear and distinct, his imagination delicate and cheerful . . ."

The humorous booklet, which quickly became popular
among the coffeehouse set, mocked the academic pretentious-
ness of Addison, Steele and their fellow literary pundits through
a series of prefaces, dedicatory poems and classical scholarship,
much of it clearly satirical. Included was the case of Ptolemaeus

Philopunnaeus, a Greek ruler who supposedly propagated a doctrine of puns in six of his major cities and ordered that every pun uttered within his dominions over the past three years be collected for his personal library.

Similarly, *Ars Punica* suggested that in the Aeolic dialect, the Greek god Pan is called Pun and that he was, in his day, a practitioner of the art. "Pan being the god of universal nature, and punning free of all languages, it is highly probable that it owes its first origin, as well as name, to this god."

Like punsters of all ages, the essay's author wrestled with the very definition of a pun and ended up offering two. The first was "The Physical Definition of Punning," describing the "art of harmonious jingling upon words, which, passing in at the ears, and falling upon the diaphragma, excites a titillary motion in those parts; and this, being conveyed by the animal spirits into the muscles of the face, raises the cockles of the heart."

The second was "The Moral Definition of Punning," which appears to be much simpler. "Punning is a virtue that most effectually promotes the end of good fellowship." But on second glance, there are two ways to interpret this: fellowship as a goal of friendship, or the termination of a friendship.

At the core of *Ars Punica* were its rules for punning. Despite the seventy-nine cited in the title, only thirty-seven were actually included, and even among these not every clause bears repeating. A few highlights, slightly paraphrased, include:

No. 8—The Rule of Interruption: Although the company may be engaged in a discourse of the most serious consequence, it is and may be lawful to interrupt them with a pun.

No. 9—The Rule of Risibility: A man must be the
first that laughs at his own pun.

No. 10—The Rule of Retaliation: If a man makes fifty
puns, you are obliged to return all, or the most of
them, in the same kind.

No. 11—The Rule of Repetition: You must never let a
pun be lost, but repeat and comment upon it, till
every one in the company both hears and under-
stands it.

No. 26—The Rule of Mortification: When a man
having got the thanks and laugh of a company for
a good pun, an enemy to the art swears he read it in
"Cambridge Jests."

Taken together, *Ars Punica*'s rules (and the puns Sheridan
offered to illustrate them) revealed a historic shift, one which
had been taking shape for several centuries but was quickly becoming codified. Essentially, after millennia in which the pun
had served as a respected rhetorical device both serious and
comic, its star was finally falling—at least in Western culture.

One factor also driving down the pun's status was a growing
British consciousness about social class. For several decades,
London's burgeoning coffeehouses had been homogenizing the
city's social interactions, casting people of widely disparate
backgrounds, professions and social status into a lively, boisterous mix. Indeed, when the coffeehouses first opened, many of
them featured seating at a long, common table—a great leveler
that forced aristocrats to face a new, more democratic reality.

Not since Geoffrey Chaucer had written his fictional (and
punning) *Canterbury Tales* in the fourteenth century had so
many people of so many different social classes been thrown

together to exchange ideas and perspectives in such a casual public forum. The resulting awareness of class difference was reflected in a growing concern about a person's accent.

Earlier in English history, strong regional accents shared roughly equal status; their differences merely reflected one's geographic origin. But as time went on and English became increasingly standardized, the upper classes began to stigmatize non-London accents and ridicule regional grammatical differences. And as a new national network of turnpikes began spreading from London like a spider's web, the capital's standards soon shaped the nation's. Puns, which often depend on stretching pronunciations and bending rules, took a corresponding hit in status.

One factor in this may have been related to England's changing standards of politeness. Early in the eighteenth century, as one scholar has written, "verbal refinement was disregarded, even among those people who had received the education of a gentleman and who were in a financial position to sustain the role and mix with good society." Public curses and insults were common, even among royalty. But that was beginning to change, and quickly. Guided by pamphlets, grammars, novels and other books instructing people in "civilized" behavior, many people began to place new value on ceremony and on what they perceived to be proper manners. From the institution of afternoon tea to the proliferation of formal toasts, standards of social propriety shifted.

One influential tastemaker was Philip Stanhope, the Fourth Earl of Chesterfield. A wealthy statesman with distinct views on what made a man a "gentleman," Lord Chesterfield wrote a series of letters to his illegitimate son explaining such behavior. When published posthumously in 1774, the letters became a de facto instruction manual for social strivers of the day.

In one such letter, he criticizes laughter itself. "I would heartily wish that you may often be seen to smile, but never heard to laugh while you live," he wrote. "Frequent and loud laughter is the characteristic of folly and ill manners; it is the manner in which the mob express their silly joy at silly things; and they call it being merry. In my mind there is nothing so illiberal, and so ill bred, as audible laughter. True wit, or sense, never made anybody laugh; they are above it." Given this attitude it's no surprise that Lord Chesterfield sniffed at puns, declaring them "not true wit" and cautioning their attempt.

Lord Chesterfield wasn't alone in looking down on the common man and his habits. The social leveling within London's coffeehouses threatened an entire strata of economic and intellectual elites, who felt that access to the pleasures of coffeehouse culture—even its wit—should not necessarily be so democratic. In their minds, intellectual banter was a privilege that required education and breeding. It was also a practice they found increasingly hard to control and, slowly but surely, the social status once associated with punning eroded. If anyone could do it, then what value did it serve as a mark of intellectual distinction? When the punning playwright William Wycherley defended punning as "a diversion," a snobby friend retorted: "I am for the Diversion of Reasonable Men and of Gentlemen. If there be any Diversion in Quibbling, it is a Diversion of which a Fool and a Porter is as capable as is the best of you."

This was about this time when the phrase "pardon the pun" began entering widespread use, an expression largely supplanted by "no pun intended" about a century later. If social strivers couldn't avoid or, more likely, resist a pun, they could at the very least offer a half-hearted apology for what was becoming more and more of a faux pas.

Of course, great and unapologetic punsters of the day were quick to defend the form and deflate such elitist pomposity. In an age when strict libel laws continued to proscribe a good deal of political speech, dramatists such as Wycherley and John Gay deliberately used puns—elusive, deniable puns—to goad and insult the powerful, who raged at such cutting satire but could do little to stop it.

Despite such efforts, the pun's status had nearly reached a tipping point. For thousands of years, the form had commanded respect for revealing divine wisdom, as a poetic expression of life's inherent contradictions, and as an elegant rhetorical tool to communicate multiple ideas at once. Now, in an Age of Reason, even the pun's most brilliant, intellectual champions were consigning it to the ghetto of humor. Soon enough, Britain's intellectual establishment piled on. In 1742, when the classical scholar Elizabeth Carter drafted a proposal for a fifteen-volume set, to be written entirely by women, of "a Most Useful and Curious Work, Entitled *The Whole Art and Mystery of Punning*," she was just being facetious.

## JOHNSON'S DICTIONARY

In 1746, a former schoolteacher named Samuel Johnson began compiling a new English dictionary. Unlike a similar project recently completed in France, in which officials had assembled a great bureaucracy to compile a French dictionary over the course of decades, Johnson undertook his project largely alone, with the assistance of only a handful of clerks. His goal? To catalog, standardize and stabilize English after several centuries of dramatic flux, in which thousands of foreign loan words had entered daily use.

Johnson's dictionary wasn't actually the first attempt to index the English language. But in this era of increasing rationalism and rising literacy rates, his systematic and comprehensive approach to evaluating and cataloging language—including etymologies and literary quotes illustrating proper usage—was considered to be a highly innovative, "scientific" method. Some words, he warned, would be left out altogether, or slapped with a caveat. "Barbarous, or impure, words and expressions may be branded with some note of infamy, as they are carefully to be eradicated wherever they are found," he wrote.

In recruiting financial backers (including Lord Chesterfield) to support what he thought would be three years of research and writing, Johnson outlined aspects of his approach, including the thorny issue of pronunciation, "the stability of which is of great importance to the duration of a language, because the first change will naturally begin by corruptions in the living speech." One way or another, he would find a way to assert order over chaos.

Johnson and his clerks set up shop in the modest, beamed garret of a rented house on London's Gough Square. But from the beginning, Johnson's project proved a monumental challenge; the entry for the letter *A* alone ran to about a thousand words, including suggested pronunciations, definitions and examples of use.

A prisoner of his own intellectual ambitions, Johnson's obsession for linguistic rigor began taking its toll. Three years became four, then stretched to five. As the words and years added up, so did Johnson's bills. To keep creditors from seizing his possessions, he began securing the front door of his house with a heavy iron chain. The chain latched onto a heavy spiral hook, much like a massive corkscrew, that was bolted into his doorframe in his entrance hall. This made it impossible for anyone to unlatch it by "fishing" through the fanlight above the door, a small opening that was itself heavily barred to block hired urchins from slipping inside.

The greatest thief, though, was time, as six years became seven, and then eight. One can just imagine him climbing those narrow steps each morning, day after day, year after year—his advance long since spent, his frustration mounting—yet still determined, absolutely determined, to put every unruly word in its place. Given the challenge, it's no surprise that he famously disliked the slippery pun. Still, he showed remarkable restraint in the definition itself ("to use the same word at once in different senses") and moved on quickly to *Punch*.

Finally, in 1755, after nearly nine years of work and the last of his Zs, Johnson rested. Published in two massive, oversize volumes, Johnson's *Dictionary of the English Language* defined more than 42,000 words and included some 114,000 literary quotations—every one selected by Johnson himself. What had taken Johnson nearly a decade to compile was quickly and widely recognized as a triumph of the English language.

In a sense, Johnson's dictionary had "fixed" English, not by locking down meanings in perpetuity, nor even ending contemporary debate over any given word. But in breadth and depth, his opus showcased the complexity and literary richness of English for the world to see, establishing the tongue of a small island—and of a growing empire—as a language to be reckoned with. As Johnson biographer Henry Hitchings has written, the dictionary "would become an instrument of cultural imperialism, and its publication was a defining moment in the realization of what was in the eighteenth century a brand-new concept, namely Britishness."

After centuries in the shadows of other European languages, English had come of age. And though the language would (and does) continue to evolve, Johnson had managed to establish a popular and widely accepted standard by which speakers and spelling and pronunciation could be judged. Even the fact that there *was* a standard at all was a relatively new concept. Almost immediately, dictionaries that followed Johnson's—in English and other languages—were judged by the standard Johnson had established.

Today it might be hard to imagine the editor of a dictionary as a celebrity, but as the reputation of Johnson's dictionary grew and subsequent editions appeared, that's exactly what the eccentric lexicographer became. Over the ensuing years, Johnson's public image and impact grew to such an extent that, in some circles, the second half of the eighteenth century became known as "The Age of Johnson," chronicled in extraordinary detail by his friend and biographer, Thomas Boswell.

Johnson used his new bully pulpit to attack, among other perceived vices, the pun. "To trifle with the vocabulary which is the vehicle of social intercourse is to tamper with the currency of human intelligence. He who would violate the sanctities of his Mother Tongue would invade the recesses of the national till without remorse," he wrote.

It didn't matter who that violator might be, even Shakespeare. In Johnson's eight-volume collection of the Bard's plays, first published in 1765, he complained bitterly about the playwright's rampant use of puns, which he called quibbles.

"A quibble is the golden apple for which he will always turn aside from his career, or stoop from his elevation," Johnson wrote. "A quibble, poor and barren as it is, gave him such delight, that he was content to purchase it, by the sacrifice of reason, propriety and truth. A quibble was to him the fatal Cleopatra for which he lost the world, and was content to lose it."

"Puns," Johnson declared, "are the last refuge of the witless."

Except, perhaps, when he made them himself. As recounted in *The Punster's Pocket-Book or The Art of Punning*, an 1826 collection of puns, Johnson and Boswell were walking past London's Old Bailey and noticed a raucous crowd gathering. At Johnson's instigation, Boswell asked someone at the edge of the crowd what was going on. The stranger reported that a man was to be hanged. And the condemned man's name? A certain Mr. Vowel.

"Well," a satisfied Johnson replied, "it is very clear, Bozzy, that it is neither U nor I."

Apparently, Johnson had no problem with capital punishment.

Despite his popular and intellectual influence, Johnson couldn't kill the pun. Resourceful English punsters continued to make the most of their language's elasticity, and the century after Johnson's death would produce some of England's greatest punsters ever. Still, in a modernizing world of scientific classification, printing presses, rising class mobility, mass culture and the resulting conformity in taste and manners, puns were now damaged goods. Tumbling from high rhetoric to low humor, the pun's reputation, like Humpty Dumpty, would never be the same again.

## A DECLARATION OF INDEPENDENCE

Across the Atlantic, American wordsmiths were rebelling. The irreverent Benjamin Franklin, who had chosen the ironic, punning pseudonym Silence Dogood to launch his literary career, was quick to add his own name to the rebellious colonies' Declaration of Independence. On signing it in 1776, perhaps cribbing from earlier English punsters, he is said to have told the Continental Congress, "We must all hang together, or assuredly we shall all hang separately."

Franklin wasn't alone in his punning. A fine tradition of punning colonial preachers, including Cotton Mather, had long since endowed such wordplay with respectability in New England. And when the prominent Boston clergyman Mather Byles, a loyalist none too pleased with the brewing Revolution, was placed under surveillance for his political leanings, he made the best of house arrest with the glib declaration that the sentinel was merely his personal "observe-a-tory."

European colonists were not the first punsters in North America, however. Many Native Americans, including those whom early colonists encountered, were skillful punsters who often used such wordplay in storytelling and in the nicknames they gave to newcomers such as William Penn. Penn was dubbed *Onas*, the Algonquin word for "feather," the pen of his day. Subsequently, *Onas* became the generic Algonquin term for any colonial governor of Pennsylvania. Other tribes such as the Navajo, Hopi and Apache also celebrated (and continue to celebrate) a rich punning tradition.

In any case, punning flourished in the New World. In 1787, Thomas Jefferson wrote a letter to Abigail Adams that complained about the number of puns flying about at the Constitutional convention, as the delegates in Philadelphia debated how best to unite a struggling nation.

"The most remarkeable [sic] effect of this convention as yet is the number of puns and bon mots it has generated. I think were they all collected it would make a more voluminous work than the Encyclopedie. This occasion, more than any thing I have seen, convinces me that this nation is incapable of any serious effort but under the word of command. The people at large view every object only as it may furnish puns and bon mots; and I pronounce that a good punster would disarm the whole nation were they ever so seriously disposed to revolt."

Jefferson's remarks indicate that the emerging stigma associated with punning in England hadn't taken hold across the Atlantic, at least not yet. As H. L. Mencken would later note, Americans had few qualms about adapting language to their needs. If English had been "dammed up at home, so to speak, by the rise of linguistic self-consciousness," Mencken wrote, creative change "continued almost unobstructed in the colonies." In fact, early American humor deliberately celebrated the young nation's very lack of pretension; if the English thought punning was "low" humor, then perhaps punning was something to celebrate all the more.

Frontier humor, especially, made the most of misspellings, exaggerated parochial dialect and the possibilities of the tall tale—the latter a kissing cousin of the Shaggy Dog story. Davy Crockett, a legend in his own lifetime, has been described by Yale historian John Mack Faragher as a "loudmouth, braggart, punster." Whatever the truth might have been, Crockett's exaggerated, almost superhuman, reputation made him an easy target for humorists, one of whom came up with the following riddle:

"How many ears does Davy Crockett have?"
"Three—a right ear, a left ear and a wild front ear."

In the early 1830s, the last years of Crockett's life before his death at the Alamo, punning became so prolific along the eastern seaboard that the editors of Boston's *Daily Evening Transcript* decried it as an epidemic. "The language is in danger of being 'stub-twisted,'" huffed one editorial. "The original signification of words will soon be lost, if a sanitary committee be not appointed to report the punsters and disinfect them forthwith." Boys, it concluded, should be prohibited from punning and smoking alike.

## GETTING THE LAST LAUGH

As it has throughout history, punning's popularity ebbed and flowed in nineteenth-century America. It attracted its share of enthusiastic practitioners, including Henry David Thoreau, Abraham Lincoln and Alexander Graham Bell, and its famous detractors, from Noah Webster to Mark Twain.

Not all American punning was in good humor, though. In the fierce 1850 debate over slavery and its extension westward, puns became weapons of ridicule. Senator Lewis Cass of Michigan, who just two years earlier had been defeated in a run for the White House, favored letting voters in a given territory decide whether slavery should be allowed or banned. The abolitionist Congressman Horace Mann argued against allowing slavery anywhere. And when Cass mocked him in a speech, punning off his name, Mann launched a sharp counterattack.

"In his last speech, General Cass deems it not unworthy his Senatorial dignity to pun upon my name. A pun has been called 'the smallest kind of wit,' and I think the General has here produced the smallest specimens of the 'smallest kind.' Did it not occur to the General that his own name offers the most grievous temptation for punning?

"As a general rule, I contemn punning. As a malignant *attack* upon any gentleman for the accident of his name, it is wholly unpardonable. It is but barely justifiable as a *retort*. To warn the General of the dangers he encounters by indulging his love of punning I will venture to subjoin a specimen or two, of what might be easily and indefinitely extended . . ." Calling the Democratic Senator a "thistle-eating donkey," Mann proceeded to run off several insulting, punning rhymes, among them the following: "This Ass is very big. Then call him CAss; C's Roman for 100—a hundred times an Ass."

Having vented, Mann proposed a truce, suggesting that if Cass "is now disposed to say 'quits,' on the score of punning, I am; and will draw no more upon the *asinine* or *Cassinine* associations which his name suggests." Just over a decade later, Confederate troops would open fire on Fort Sumter, sparking the Civil War.


IN 1856, A BOSTON MAGAZINE CALLED *PUTNAM'S MONTHLY* PUB-lished a long essay entitled "The Philosophy of Punning." Apparently, most Americans of the era still viewed punning as a sign of intellectual creativity and distinction, and a talent to strive for and share with pride.

"The pun flourishes among the toasts and sentiments of the land," the author wrote. "There is scarcely a festive gathering on which that cheerful equivocation will not be found sparkling amidst the regulated or volunteer sententiousness of the occasion."

The pun, according to the author, served an important purpose. "Almost all the conceivable toasts and sentiments in the world—social, political, warlike, agrarian, commercial, chivalrous, and so forth—are worn threadbare with frequent use, and it asks a vast deal of ingenuity well expended, to find some new, neat way of saying what has been often said already. Here the pun comes in very well, throwing a genial flash of hilarity over scenes that, between ourselves, often stand in need of it. Our puns are protests against the trite and the prolix, and a wholesome recognition of the popular taste."

Genial hilarity? A protest against the trite? By today's standards, that's high praise for the lowly pun.

Today, even those who like puns are prone to think of them as "corny" humor. But the meaning of corny is one whose roots leave many tasseled etymologists furrowing their brows. Several possibilities stand out. Most likely, in an urbanizing society, corny might have been a derogative way to describe the humor of farmers (and other newcomers to the city) as unsophisticated.

Alternatively, the British lexicographer Eric Partridge noted in his 1937 dictionary of slang and unconventional English that the term is a variation on *corned*, meaning "drunk," and applied to mean "*pickled* and *salted* for semantics."

Still another, more remote, possibility might derive from Oxford's Cornmarket Street, long ago nicknamed "The Corn" by carousing undergraduates. As a university town noted for its enthusiastic punsters (not to mention the hapless Archibald Spooner), "corny" humor might have originated among grain farmers trading the latest jokes, which were then quickly propagated by students.

Another derogatory term often applied to puns is "cheesy." But in the 1850s, calling something cheesy meant that it was in fashion, correct, showy, or fine. Does this then mean that all puns, one way or another, must really be Gouda?

ONE NINETEENTH-CENTURY CHAMPION OF THE PUN, LARGELY forgotten today, was William Mathews. In addition to teaching English at the University of Chicago, he authored a series of self-help books in the 1870s and 1880s, including *Wit and Humor: Their Use and Abuse.* In this 1888 bestseller, Mathews devotes a long chapter to Puns and Punsters. Citing the pun's classical roots and illustrious past, Mathews decried the "atrabilious jesticide" of the pun's critics.

While conceding that the "professional punster" who lies in wait for easy prey is a "cold-blooded, hardened wretch," he praised the impromptu humorist whose puns preceded more serious subjects, like "the froth and sparkle of champagne before wines with more body."

"Why it should provoke such hostility when legitimately employed, is an enigma hard to explain. There are few persons who do not betray, if they do not avow, a keen relish for this species of jest, when it is used sparingly and is really extempore," he wrote.

Mathews, the Dale Carnegie of his day, argued that more effective use of language could solve many, if not most, problems. In his mind, a perfect pun was no lemon to be swallowed in bitterness, but rather an opportunity that, when ripe, was pithy and potentially sublime. "Words are often not only the vehicle of

thought," he wrote, "but the very mirror in which we see our
ideas, and behold the beauty or ugliness of our inner selves."


## JEWISH WRY

As the twentieth century approached, though, American attitudes toward punning began to shift. All across the country,
but most acutely along the eastern seaboard, Americans were
confronting the challenges of industrialization, urbanization
and massive immigration. Between 1880 and 1920 nearly 24
million immigrants arrived in the United States. Unlike earlier
newcomers, who had come largely from countries in western
and northern Europe, this latest wave hailed primarily from
southern and eastern Europe. Among other impacts, this shift
would inevitably influence America's sense of humor. Like earlier arrivals, many of these immigrants were punsters, as nearly
all cultures play with language to some degree. That said, one
particular group of immigrants stood out in this regard: Jews.

From the dawn of their religion, Jews have focused intensely
on language, and textual analysis in particular, starting with
the Ten Commandments. In the original Hebrew, the Old Testament itself is full of wordplay in general and puns specifically.
In 1894 Immanuel Moses Casanowicz, a doctoral candidate at
Johns Hopkins University, actually tabulated such wordplay
page by page in a dissertation entitled *Paronomasia In The Old
Testament* (Paronomasia is a classical term of rhetoric that en-
compasses punning).

One biblical pun that Casanowicz identifies appears in the
Book of Job, when the beleaguered, frustrated protagonist suggests to God that "perhaps thou hast mistaken *iyob* (Job) for

*oyeb* (enemy)." It's not a knee-slapper by any stretch, but at the time, puns weren't expected to pull the cart of humor. In a similar spirit, scholars who followed Casanowicz have discovered that the Book of Job and other books in the Hebrew Bible are rich with so-called Janus Parallels. This is a poetic device in which a punning word, through one of its meanings, echoes the content of the preceding line and, through its second meaning, previews the line to follow.

Given the frequency and richness of biblical puns, it's not surprising that the Babylonian Talmud, an ancient compilation of rabbinic commentaries on Jewish theology, law, ethics, history and philosophy, also includes its share of puns. This makes sense, because puns were sometimes a useful way of incorporating, or reconciling, different ideas contained within a single word or phrase. In any case, over the centuries, this Jewish passion for textual analysis and the constant struggle for survival helped shape the wry, highly verbal, Jewish sense of humor.

For an ancient example, consider the Jewish revolt against Roman occupiers in the second century AD. At the time, some rabbis came to believe that the revolt's charismatic leader, Simon ben Kosiba, was the Messiah. Playing off the letters of his name, they endowed him with a punning nickname (which doesn't survive transliteration) meaning Son of the Star.

For six years, ben Kosiba and his rebel soldiers gave the best Roman troops a run for their money. Archeological evidence indicates that his forces controlled a good deal of Judea, and for long enough, to issue their own coinage. Ultimately, though, the Romans finally cornered and defeated Simon ben Kosiba in AD 136, at which point the fallen leader got a new punning nickname of Simon bar Koziva, meaning "son of the lie."

A thousand years later Jews were still being persecuted, and still punning. In the Middle Ages, the tradition of Talmudic punning gave rise to the so-called Purim Torah of Eastern Europe. These were humorous, often punning parodies of Talmudic scholarship composed to mark the holiday of Purim, which commemorates the Jews' triumph over their would-be Persian annihilators, as recorded in the Book of Esther.

By the late nineteenth century, humorous puns had taken root in secular Jewish writing, popularized by bestselling Yiddish authors and playwrights such as Solomon Naumovich Rabinovich, better known by his pen name, Sholem Aleichem, Yiddish for "Peace Be With You." Yiddish, like English, is a hybrid of other languages. As such, it's rich in homophones that make for easy punning. Aleichem, who is most famous today for writing the stories that were immortalized in *Fiddler on the Roof,* used puns cleverly and ironically. Many were never intended to be "ha-ha" funny, but rather "ah-ha" clever. Unfortunately, it's very difficult to cite an example that survives translation with any semblance of grace.

At this time, in Aleichem's Ukraine and throughout Eastern Europe, anti-Semitism was on the rise. Following the assassination of Tsar Alexander II in 1881, a wave of bloody pogroms against Jews sparked massive emigration westward. Millions of Jews, Aleichem among them, packed up and left their native lands: some to England and Palestine, some to South America, and more than a million to the United States. They couldn't carry much in their bundles and their steamer trunks, but they did bring their love of language.

In New York City and elsewhere, these homesick immigrants were soon flocking to Yiddish theaters, in dire need of familiar entertainment and a good laugh. Typically ironic, wry and often flowing from the bitterness of experience, such humor had long helped Jews cope when times were tough. Naturally, sympathetic immigrant audiences reacted accordingly, sometimes laughing, sometimes groaning.

Ruth Wisse is the Martin Peretz Professor of Yiddish Literature and a Professor of Comparative Literature at Harvard, and an expert on Aleichem's work. In a 2010 interview in *The Jewish Week*, she explained that "Yiddish humor is insider humor. It's very much based on Jewish sources, and the better you know the sources, the funnier the puns are."

Soon enough, English-speaking Jewish comedians were playing to mainstream audiences and punning to great effect. After all, Americans of diverse backgrounds had long embraced puns and were hungry for fresh talent. In the first half of the twentieth century, many Jewish comedians—Jack Benny, the Marx Brothers, Henny Youngman, Milton Berle, Gracie Allen and George Burns among them—rose to prominence. It wasn't that Jewish comedians were the only punsters: Charlie Chaplin, Laurel & Hardy and Abbott & Costello were masters of the art as well. From Vaudeville to Broadway to Hollywood, puns were stock in trade.

Sometime around mid-century, though, the public's changing comedic tastes began to maroon the humble pun. Although the precise tipping point is hard to pinpoint, puns began to draw more and more groans. Postwar audiences didn't reject the pun entirely, but began responding better to humor that was a little more raw and a little less obviously constructed.

In an atomic age of duck-and-cover, the McCarthy hearings, and a nagging ennui about suburban conformism, a new and more irreverent stream of consciousness began to gather force. Much as jazz audiences of the time embraced the more dissonant music of Miles Davis, John Coltrane and Thelonious

Monk, edgier comedic audiences were applauding iconoclastic Jewish comics such as Woody Allen and Lenny Bruce who, starting in the 1950s, began challenging longstanding humorous forms and taboos.

While both of them appreciated wordplay and Bruce pushed public language to new frontiers of impropriety, they drove American comedy in a whole new direction, away from the standard joke-and-punch-line routines. Other great comics quickly followed suit, and as the 1960s gathered momentum, traditional comedy began to seem passé, especially if audiences considered the topic to be tame. As such, the popularity of puns took a dive. One might argue that this decline is reflected in the self-deprecating title of the 1968 book *Bennett Cerf's Treasury of Atrocious Puns*. In literature, "treasury" often suggests that something is old-fashioned, as if its contents were forever locked in the amber of nostalgia. Yet, if Cerf's book contained its share of old chestnuts, many of its puns were actually quite clever. Despite this, Cerf, a well-respected TV personality and the founder of Random House, felt compelled to label them all as "atrocious."

It was a sign of the times. In this new age of sex, drugs, profanity and rebellion, tens of millions of Americans were embracing a more free-form humor that celebrated dysfunction and cynicism, not the traditional schtick. When self-proclaimed atheist George Carlin first recorded his monologue "Seven Words You Can Never Say on Television" in 1972, it was a defiant political statement on freedom of speech. When he tried to perform it live in Milwaukee, local police arrested him.

In such a charged environment, puns weren't considered subversive enough. At a time in which social and cultural and political institutions, even the presidency, seemed to be coming apart at the seams, the pun had become something of an automatic groaner, unless you were very old or very young.

As always, though, there were exceptions. One was the manic, punning wordplay of Alan Alda's Hawkeye Pierce on *M\*A\*S\*H*, the sitcom set in wartime Korea which—as an allegory on the Vietnam war—became a runaway hit in the 1970s and early 1980s. The army doctors he and his costars played "were trying to maintain their sanity by acting crazy," Alda later explained.

More directly, comedian Johnny Carson continued to work occasional puns into *The Tonight Show*, often during his "Carnac the Magnificent" routine. Wearing a feathered turban and a cape, Carson would divine the answer to an unknown question that had been sealed in an envelope, then open the envelope to "prove" his magical abilities. They often turned on a pun. If the answer were "innuendo," the question might be "What's an Italian word for suppository?"

Such clever, unexpected puns still had the power to draw laughs, both publicly and privately. One man who loved them was Ed Muskie, the U.S. Senator from Maine who ran a strong campaign for the Democratic presidential nomination in 1972. According to his aide Lester Hyman, Muskie had a good sense of humor. Still, in the brutal back-and-forth of a presidential campaign, laughter was in short supply. As Hyman recounted in an online memoir, Muskie was campaigning in New York City one day, and was being picketed by loud, angry activists who wanted him to make a public statement in support of gay rights.

Despite Hyman's urging that issuing a generic statement on Constitutional freedoms and privacy would suffice, Muskie—a progressive who feared the potential political cost—refused. As

Muskie and Hyman got into their car, the protesters surrounded the vehicle and started rocking it back and forth, yelling.

"What do they want?" an agitated Muskie asked.

Hyman leaned in and whispered: "They want to fuck you, Ed!"

Muskie roared with laughter, and later released a statement on the issue.

Invariably, humor is subjective. It involves myriad social, linguistic and other variables, many of which change over time. That's what makes it so challenging to define or describe in the abstract. According to laughter researcher Robert Provine, studies have shown that "laughter doesn't equal humor, and humor doesn't equal laughter."

Provine argues that this common misperception has been unduly influenced by the rise of stand-up comedy. He notes that such routines are often driven by a series of jokes delivered at some distance by a deadpan comedian, which bears very little relation to laughter as we experience it in everyday life. In reality, his field observations reveal that most laughter in ordinary conversation is not generated by jokes at all. Rather, people laugh for a variety of reasons, and hearing something funny is only one of them. People might also laugh to show subservience to those of greater power or prestige, or because others around them are laughing and they want to fit in. It is this group psychology that (in addition to lower costs) helped give rise to the recorded laugh track.

In any case, while the public reputation of puns continued to fall through the second half of the twentieth century, the reality of punning's role in daily intercourse remained far more complex.

## TO GROAN, OR NOT TO GROAN

No exploration of the tumultuous relationship between puns and humor would be complete without taking a closer look at the ritual groan that many people, on hearing a pun, feel compelled to utter. Those who tend to groan or otherwise protest every pun will often argue that their response is a universal and appropriate reflex to a particularly "low" form of humor. This is a cultural myth on both counts.

As the lexicographer Henry Fowler noted in his classic *Modern English Usage*, "The assumption that puns are *per se* contemptible, betrayed by the habit of describing every pun not as 'a pun' but as 'a bad pun' or 'a feeble pun,' is a sign at once of sheepish docility and a desire to seem superior. Puns are good, bad, and indifferent, and only those who lack the wit to make them are unaware of the fact."

Fowler, who wrote that in 1926, was absolutely correct. And if you pay close attention to how people actually respond to puns in daily life, you'll notice that, depending on the context, puns elicit a wide range of responses—most of them positive.

First, consider the puns that permeate rap. The rapper André 3000, of OutKast, explained his decision to get married with the following verse: "So, I typed a text to a girl I used to see / sayin' that I chose this cutie pie with whom I wanna be / and I apologize if this message gets you down / Then I CC'd every girl that I'd see-see 'round town." To millions of fans, such punning sparks neither laughter nor groans, just more sales.

Like their rap counterparts, country music fans don't tend to groan at puns, either. If they did, why would Nashville songwriters employ them so often in the genre's lyrics and titles? Consider Mel Street, who laments lost love in "Looking Out

My Window Through the Pain." Similarly, the Statler Brothers sang about a man on a double date at a drive-in movie who goes to buy popcorn and returns to find his buddy in the backseat, enjoying the pleasures of both women at once. The song's title? "You Can't Have Your Kate and Edith Too."

More subtle is Johnny Cash's "Folsom Prison Blues." When he played to the convicted felons at California's Folsom State Prison in 1968, his lyrics referenced the blues in more ways than one—not just the inmates' incarceration, but their mandatory blue uniforms, too.

Puns also fare well on Broadway. Year after year in midtown Manhattan, large audiences pay top dollar for clever wordplay, especially in musical theater. In shows from Gershwin to Sondheim, puns have long played a critical if understudied role, and help earn rave reviews. Even the oldest, most familiar puns still draw legions of fans, as thousands wait hours in line for free tickets to see Shakespeare in the Park, groaning only when the tickets run out.

Yet another audience that doesn't groan at puns is children, many of whom delight in knock-knock jokes and punning riddles. "What's black and white and red all over?" has been kicking about American and British schoolyards since at least the middle of the 1800s. Others have had their day and disappeared: "Why did the window box? Because it saw the garden fence" or "Why did the jam roll? Because it saw the apple turnover." A perennial favorite among precocious three- and four-year-olds remains "What do a tree, an elephant and a car all have in common? Trunks."

Regardless of the specific joke, the effect of such preschool and playground puns is consistent over time: glee at the discovery that one can play with language, turn sense into nonsense, and nonsense into sense. And it's this very wordplay that exposes children to the mechanics of semantics, long before they ever tackle grammar in a classroom.

Studies also indicate that children's facility with language has a major impact on their ability to excel in other subjects, too, including math and science. Playing with language helps them discover similarities, differences and patterns, as well as how to make bold conceptual leaps, as the following schoolyard ditty illustrates:

> Mississippi said to Missouri
> If I put on my New Jersey
> What will Delaware?
> Virginia said, Alaska.

Such wordplay is far from simple, requiring the ability to shift frames of reference in rapid succession, from place to person to object to action. That's why, from *Sesame Street* to *Mad Magazine* to the Muppets, puns are tools that engage, educate and entertain. Not just the young, either, but the young at heart. Just who, watching old clips on YouTube, can resist laughing as a startled Rudolf Nureyev finds himself dancing with Miss Piggy in *Swine Lake*, the balletic tale of a princess-turned-porker, trapped by the spell of the wicked magician Trichinosis?

"We do comedy, just like Monty Python," said Kirk Thatcher, a longtime Muppet writer and director. "You don't want to leave the kids out, and you don't want to exclude the adults."

And despite the virtual disappearance of puns in most modern stand-up routines, other forms of comedy are overflowing with puns and to great comic effect. Do people typically groan at all the puns that pepper reruns of *The Flintstones, Gilligan's Island*, James Bond movies or the 1980 slapstick classic *Airplane*? Surely not. Contemporary shows are full of puns, too. Consider *The Simpsons* and *Family Guy*. Their sharp social commentary, rich with puns, tends to make people smile, chuckle or laugh out loud. And if people do groan, it's usually driven by a sense of irony, not the puns.

Slyly, the G-rated *SpongeBob SquarePants* lives in a place called Bikini Bottom, and in *Austin Powers: The Spy Who Shagged Me*, Austin is anything but clandestine when it comes to his puns. Meeting a scantily clad villain who introduces herself as Ivana Humpalot, he responds "I vanna toilet made out of solid gold, but it's just not in the cards now, is it?" Again, such punning doesn't draw groans; it gets audiences roaring and sells millions of tickets.

What about all those puns in daily headlines? The impetus is partly practical: trying to pack as much meaning as possible into just a few words is not just a challenge, it's something of an art. When the *New York Post* announced deposed Iraqi Dictator Saddam Hussein's execution, it conveyed not just the news but also an editorial opinion in its front-page headline, GOOD NOOSE. The impetus for such punning is also commercial. Catchy headlines sell papers, and the New York tabloids often compete to out-pun each other in daily headline wars. Some trace the proliferation of such headlines in New York tabloids to the outsized influence of *Post* owner Rupert Murdoch, who's not afraid to offend anyone.

In *Headless Body in Topless Bar*, a collection of *New York Post* headlines, newsman Robert Walsh writes that "Nothing gives me greater satisfaction than watching someone thumbing through *The Post* on the subway and breaking into a smile, almost on cue, when he or she turns a page and is immediately tickled by one of the heads. That's my silent fist-pump 'Yes' moment."

Even the staid *New York Times* allows that occasional wordplay is not all bad. According to the paper's style guide, "puns have a place in the paper, but as a trace element rather than a staple. A pun should be a surprise encounter, evoking a sly smile rather than a groan, and flattering the intelligence of a reader who gets the joke. Plays on personal names never qualify: no one will be flattered to read, say, that a pitcher named Butcher *carved up* the opposing team. The successful pun pivots on a word that fits effortlessly into two contexts. . . . The more obvious kind of wordplay (*Rubber Industry Bounces Back*) should be tested on a trusted colleague the way mine shaft air is tested on a canary. When no song bursts forth, start rewriting."

Joe Lapointe, a longtime sportswriter at the paper, laments that the canaries rarely sing from the skyscraper on West Fortieth Street. "You send them anyway to see if they'll shoot them down, and 99% of the time they do," he said. "Even William Shakespeare couldn't get his puns past our copy desk."

But sometimes, a pun is so clever that even *The Times* can't resist using it in a headline. In 2009, it ran a snippet about a man who attended a Spanish jazz festival and filed a complaint with local police over the performance of a band. His allegation? He didn't think their music qualified as jazz. The headline? OFFICER, THAT'S NOT JAZZ, I SAY, IT'S FELONIOUS JUNK! More recently, the paper ran a story about President Obama's redecoration of the Oval Office, with a headline reading THE AUDACITY OF TAUPE.

Actually, the *Times* runs puns in one form or another almost every day, in its famous crossword puzzle. Its clues and answers often depend on them. Puns are also the hallmark of many greeting cards (a trend that began in the early 1900s, and continues today). In short, whether they appear in crosswords or kind words, people are almost always happy to get the pun. Even *The New Yorker* has begun to pun. Topping a recent review of former British Prime Minister Tony Blair's autobiography was the headline WHICH BLAIR PROJECT, a pun on *The Blair Witch Project*, the 1999 horror film. And to embellish a 2010 essay by Woody Allen, the magazine ran an illustration of a cow and the headline UDDER MADNESS. From beyond the grave, William Shawn might just agree.

Puns aren't just food for thought, either. Walk the aisles of a supermarket, and you'll find puns there, too. Sun-Maid Raisins, Ben & Jerry's Karamel Sutra and Cherry Garcia ice creams, and Pup-Peroni dog treats, among others. Trader Joe's, especially, revels in punning signage. Perhaps that's because puns sell products. A 2004 study by Dutch researchers found that consumers actually preferred punning product slogans over those without puns. Even when consumers examined slogans without puns, they still preferred those in which they *perceived* a pun. According to the data, the more legitimate meanings a punning slogan managed to integrate, the better.

Similarly, churches today are punning to sell their services, too. In a culture where even God has to compete for time and attention, houses of worship across the United States have been posting catchy phrases on their exterior signboards. "God Answers Knee-Mail," and "Life Stinks: We Have a Pew for You," and "Son Screen Prevents Sin Burn," are just a few. And for happy sinners? They can put their money on horses with names like Dangling Chad, Don't Countess Out, or Mascarponi. Whoever wins, they'll get their just desserts.

Finally, even comedians will still work in the occasional pun, as long as it flows naturally and doesn't feel too contrived, according to Frank Santopadre, a comedy writer who has written for Bill Murray, Dennis Miller and, currently, Joy Behar.

He cites Dennis Miller's joke (not one he wrote) about a female teacher arrested for sex with a student. Miller complains to his audience, saying "When I was in school, the only thing I got to do was bang the erasers." People roared with laughter.

Taken together, these diverse examples suggest that—contrary to the common stereotype—groaning in response to a pun is neither automatic nor universal. And when people do groan, that response can mean many things.

So just when exactly *do* people groan at puns, and what *does* it mean? Sociologists at Central Michigan University who actually studied the pun-related groan determined that it's not necessarily related to a given pun's cleverness or banality. Rather, it's often triggered by the mere fact that, under certain conditions, someone has made an obvious and deliberate pun. Of course, there isn't a punster alive who needs to read *Studies in Symbolic Interaction* to know this.

Some people will argue that when it comes to puns, a groan is high praise. That's not necessarily true. Sometimes a groan is a compliment, sometimes it isn't, and sometimes it's neither. The truth is, when people hear a pun and actually groan, that response can spring from several distinct urges. These include the listener's desire to acknowledge that he or she got the joke, however lame; irritation at having been momentarily taken in by the punster's verbal subterfuge; displeasure at a punster's perceived overreach; frustration at the punster for interrupting the listener's train of thought; a desire to discourage further punning; or even to disguise the fact that he or she didn't actually get the joke.

Comedian Gilbert Gottfried suggests that some people groan to demonstrate their superiority. "People want to show they're a lot more intelligent or above something," he said. Much as rippling laughter can be contagious in an audience, he said, so can groans. Michael Barrie, a comedy writer who has collaborated with everyone from Dean Martin to Johnny Carson to David Letterman, said that the groan "comes out of the terminal irony we're stuck in now."

Incidentally, both irony and sarcasm are, like puns, a way to say one thing and mean another. However, irony and sarcasm don't suffer the pun's poor reputation. Maybe this is because punning, which seeks to create a connection between words or ideas, is inherently an attempt at intellectual construction. Irony and sarcasm, by contrast, tend to be acts of criticism or destruction. Generally speaking, it's much harder to create than to criticize, and so fewer people are willing to take the risk. This may explain why many people arbitrarily prefer irony and sarcasm to punning, because they're easier and safer. Which isn't to say that one can't be creative and funny with irony or sarcasm, as Jerry Seinfeld has proven to hilarious effect.

In addition to conveying criticism, a groan can also signal a listener's grudging admiration of a pun's cleverness, or even reflect someone's need to suppress deserved praise because to praise a pun outright would violate a common social norm. As the retired Borscht Belt comedian and actor Mickey Freeman explains: "When they're good, they get a groan; when they're bad, they get the same kind of recognition." Years earlier, Milton Berle suggested yet another reason: "The groans that greet such puns are usually envious," he said. "The other person wishes he had said it."

One can even imagine situations in which the groan is a combination of several overlapping, even competing impulses, both positive and negative. Perhaps that's one reason why people groan—because it's a quick, convenient shorthand for conveying a tangle of emotions. Physiologically, it might even be the product of a brain toggling so fast, and so inconclusively, that it can't decide what to verbalize.

Gary Hallock is the longtime producer and emcee of the annual O. Henry Pun-Off World Championships and an Austin, Texas, property manager who likes to joke that he's "spent 20 years on the pun-employment line here." A former champion himself, he acknowledges that most punsters expect and accept a groan in response to their puns, sometimes even claiming it as a backhanded compliment. But that attitude is really just an emotional shield for self-defense, Hallock said. What many punsters really seek, he added, is the validation of laughter. And for one afternoon each May in Austin, Texas, the very best punsters get a lot of it from the crowd that gathers to watch the contest.

"The Pun-Off is the one time of the year in which you can expect true appreciation instead of being treated like a pariah," he said. "Sure, you hear a lot of bad, dull, pedestrian puns. But when someone pulls off something in the moment, in context and on topic, people will stand up and cheer. That's the reaction that all punsters crave."

If the meaning of a groan can be ambiguous, however, the verbal rimshot—commonly phrased as some variant of "ba-dump-bump!" and often pantomimed with imaginary drumsticks—is never mistaken for anything but sarcastic criticism. A surly cousin of the groan, the rimshot is named for the way in which drummers strike the metal rim of their snare-drum at the same time they strike its skin. Like the percussive flourish that drummers in the house bands of late-night talk shows often unleash following a comedian's failed joke, the verbal rimshot is acoustic shorthand for "Hey, I got your 'joke,' but it's not funny."

It wasn't always so. In the days of Vaudeville, according to comedy writer, director and producer Alan Kirschenbaum, the drummer's rimshot was used to punctuate a good joke, not poke fun at it. It was a cue for laughter, not derision. It was only in the 1950s that the rimshot acquired its current, derogatory meaning.

## THE COMEBACK

After suffering a long decline in its public reputation, the pun seems to be making something of a comeback. Consider the popular (RED) campaign, launched in 2006, to support the global fight against AIDS, tuberculosis and malaria. This on-going effort enlists diverse companies to raise public awareness and money by marketing goods and services connected with the color or word red. Examples include red T-shirts printed with the words Inspi(Red), a British floral delivery service called Flowe(Red), and a series of bumper stickers that, to pro-test the high price of AIDS drugs, declared the major drug companies to be P(RED)ATORS. As of 2010, the campaign had raised $150 million.

Similarly, ads and titles for movies and TV shows often pun with abandon. One recent example is *Hung*, an HBO comedic drama about a struggling high school teacher who moonlights as a male prostitute. Its tagline? Back to the grind. Others include the ABC hospital drama *Scrubs,* the series of *Legally Blonde* movies, the 2007 animated feature film *Ratatouille* (about a French rat that dreams of becoming a chef), and the 2010 movie *Cats & Dogs: The Revenge of Kitty Galore.* Kitty Galore is, like Austin Powers' Ivana Humpalot, a pun on a pun (Pussy Galore) from *Goldfinger,* the 1964 James Bond film. Even *Sex and the City*, with all its double entendres, gets into the act.

Meanwhile, if one needs a haircut, a pedicure or even just a soothing oatmeal bath, there are now nearly two thousand salons in the United States named A Cut Above, Shear Magic or Mane Event to meet that need. Just be sure to double-check before the appointment, though, as many of these establishments cater to customers with four legs, not two.

Or consider the New York frozen dessert company Tasti D Lite, which trademarked the pun "dessert your guilt." Dunkin' Donuts, similarly, advertises the presence of its ATMs with window stickers that ask: "Need Some Dough? ATM Inside." In a similar spirit, the Chipotle restaurant chain issues receipts that proclaim "Life is burritoful." Meanwhile, across the pond, Jamie Oliver, Britain's Naked Chef, sells a line of personal home consumer products under the brand "Jme."

There's Counter Culture Coffee, Bean and Gone, and Sacred Grounds. There's also the Pluck U chicken franchise and Chili Today-Hot Tamale, a New Jersey chili powder and snack company. If you want Greek food in downtown Indianapolis, try Aesop's Tables. Or if you're passing through Evanston, Illinois, and suddenly hunger for a hot dog, why not squeeze in lunch at Mustard's Last Stand? Alternatively, in Key West, Florida, there's a Caribbean jerk joint called Jamaican Me Hungry.

If you're chilly and looking for cashmere, try the line from Knit Wit. Or if you're shopping on New York City's Bleecker Street, stop into the women's clothing boutique Olive & Bette's; its canvas shopping bag depicts a stuffed olive as the *O* in the phrase "Olive You"—a verbal, visual and aural pun all at once.

Finally, if you want to get away from it all, just walk the docks of virtually any marina. Chances are, you're likely to spot pun after pun, with yachts or fishing boats named *Reel Time*, *Better Knot*, *Between the Sheets* and many more. The bottom line is that, once you start paying attention, you'll find puns almost everywhere.

That said, whether any given pun is clever, funny or neither always depends on the audience. Consider the Michigan company that, some years ago, emblazoned the doors of its portable toilets with the phrase "Here's Johnny!" For Tonight Show fans who encountered them, the facilities were probably good for a yuk in more ways than one.

Johnny Carson, though, didn't like being the butt of the joke. Catching wind of the toilets, Carson filed suit in Federal Court, alleging that the company had—in appropriating Ed McMahon's exuberant, nightly introduction—violated both his right to privacy and so-called "right of publicity."

If we set aside all legal arguments, it says a lot that such a lawsuit, *John Carson and Johnny Carson Apparel, Inc. v. Here's Johnny Portable Toilets, Inc.* was ever filed in the first place. Number one, the case highlighted how extraordinarily litigious modern society had become. And number two, the lawsuit reaffirmed the enduring, subversive power of humor in general, and puns in particular. Yes, the law has always been an argument about the precise meaning of words, which are often crude articulations of broader concepts. But when a popular comedian sues a portable toilet company over a puerile pun and the defendant's law firm is Krass & Young, the absurdity almost becomes meta-humor.

After a long paper chase, Carson prevailed. It was the only time in history that a comedian with a full house beat an opponent's royal flush.

# CHAPTER 4

*Riddles of History:
How Puns Conquered
Human Imagination*

LIKE THE JEWELS OF AN EMERALD NECKLACE, THE LUSH ISLANDS of the Hawaiian archipelago stretch across 1,500 miles of open ocean. According to the Kumulipo, the sacred Hawaiian Song of Creation, the gods lifted these idyllic islands from the watery depths and, night by night, created all known life. Passed down as a chant from generation to generation, the Kumulipo first came to western attention in 1881, when a former ship's doctor turned anthropologist, Adolf Bastian, published a partial translation. Despite his efforts, many of the oral epic's nuances were lost, in part due to the chant's prolific use of Hawaiian puns.

As the late anthropologist Martha Beckwith wrote of the Kumulipo, the "use of a double meaning in a word extends to whole passages. A vivid description of natural scenes or activities, some mood of nature or . . . of myth, may conceal an allusion recognized by the native listener but wholly misinterpreted by us of another culture who attempt translation."

This love of symbolism and hidden meaning is found throughout Polynesia, and has probably been a part of Hawaiian culture since lost or intrepid voyagers, perhaps from Tahiti or the Marquesas Islands, first stepped ashore about 1,600 years ago. In fact, well beyond the Kumulipo, Hawaiian legend is rich with riddles and wordplay. According to island lore, rivals often settled disputes by means of a riddling contest, challenging each other with conundrums built upon deep local knowledge and intricate wordplay. Making and catching sophisticated puns was often critical to victory, and such punning exchanges weren't intended to be funny. In extreme cases, losers even paid with their lives.

In one such fable, a renowned riddler from Hawaii challenged the Chief of Kauai, and bet his life on the outcome. He lost, and his bones were left to bleach in the sun. His young son Kalapana, who was short and fat and ridiculed by his playmates, was determined to avenge his father. His mother, unable to dissuade him, sent the boy to train with her older sister, who was wise in the ancient art. After months of practice, he hoisted the sail on his outrigger and pushed off the beach at Hilo. Guided by the sun and the stars, he set course for Kauai, some three hundred miles away.

Weeks later, when Kalapana stepped ashore at Kauai and announced his challenge, the Chief and his followers were contemptuous. Who was this fat little boy, this impudent son of a failure? Inside the ritual riddling house, they all jeered and refused him entrance. But the Chief's younger brother, who believed in fair play, took up his cause. Since the boy had braved the dangerous seas, didn't he at least deserve a chance to confront his nemesis? Grudgingly, they invited him inside.

Kalapana had come prepared for an unforgiving contest, and began to unpack his riddler's calabash, a large gourd that had kept his gear dry during the voyage. Some of what he brought was practical, and some was for show; in a hostile environment, he was determined not to be shamed. Among other items he brought a sleeping mat, a block of *wili-wili* wood for a pillow, fishing line, fire sticks and kindling, dried meat, a water bottle and *awa* root (used to fight migraines), a black beach stone, a smooth pebble, extra loincloths, a stone hatchet and an array of dried fish with mystical, punning names.

Seeing Kalapana settling in for a comfortable stay, the Chief's nine advisors decided to get the contest over with, and announced the terms. Before he could take on the Chief, he would have to outwit the entire council, one by one. The penalty for defeat? Death by dismemberment.

One by one, the nine squared off against Kalapana. One by one, they fell before his punning wit and were hacked to pieces. When the Chief's turn came, he, too, was out-riddled, and met the same bloody fate. Only the Chief's younger brother, the one who had insisted on fair play, was left unharmed. Then Kalapana, having avenged his father, calmly packed up his calabash, walked down the beach to his outrigger and—never having lowered his sail—shoved off into the surf and on toward home.

Such verbal sparring and the puns on which they turn are not just the stuff of ancient legend. Even today, such punning is found around the globe in various forms, from Balinese clown banter to oral poetry duels at traditional Palestinian weddings to the back-and-forth of Japanese *manzai* comedy.

Sometimes the exchange of puns is completely silent, but no less clever. In Nigeria, a primitive form of text messaging is sometimes practiced by young lovers communicating their affections by sending strings of cowry shells back and forth. Six on a string means "I like you," because the Yoruba word for six also sounds like the word for "attracted." Receiving a string of eight cowries in return would be a welcome reply, because the word for eight also sounds like the word for "agreed."

One especially rich tradition of punning duels can be found in the Chiapas highlands of southern Mexico, in and around the market town of San Juan de Chamula. It is only four hundred miles away from Mexico City but, culturally and politically, it stands a world apart. One manifestation of this gulf is the fact that more than 329,000 people from Chiapas don't claim Spanish as their first language. They speak various dialects of Tzotzil, an indigenous Mayan language that long predates the sixteenth-century arrival of Spanish conquistadores.

The Maya, whose civilization reached its cultural, economic and political peak between AD 250–900, apparently loved puns. The evidence? Carved hieroglyphs with multiple meanings—some serious, some humorous. According to Maya legend, all people originally spoke the same language. Inevitably, though, they began squabbling. This upset the sun god who, in an attempt to make peace, separated them into groups, each with their own language. Those near San Juan Chamula were given "true language" and have honored that gift ever since by promoting and celebrating both eloquence and verbal games.

One way Chamulan men do this is through the ritualized verbal duels involving riddles, jokes, proverbs, lies and insults, many of which hinge on clever puns. Such humorous verbal duels are called *k'ehel k'op*.

According to anthropologist Gary Gossen, a young Chamulan man might challenge another to match wits by slinging a playful insult: "Hang your carrying bag over your shoulder well, because I see that it is falling off." In the local dialect, the statement is charged, because all men and boys more than ten years old are expected to carry a *moral*—a shoulder bag (or, if they have only a plastic bag, to carry it by hand). But the word *moral* has another meaning, too: scrotum. As such, Gossen writes, the speaker might be suggesting that his target's private parts are visible, or that he is effeminate.

As Gossen notes, the man accused of mishandling or missing his bag "will not be embarrassed, but will simply laugh and answer the challenge with a friendly grab at the accuser's genitals; then the accuser will probably return the grab." Alternatively, the original target "may also answer the verbal challenge with another pun which will put the original accuser on the defensive to come up with still another line in the verbal duel." Some of these *k'ehel k'op* duels last for hundreds of exchanges, and enable participants to obliquely address sensitive topics, such as romantic relationships, through the safe exchange of salty humor. Not all *k'ehel k'op* duels feature puns or even quasi-erotic come-ons, but Gossen notes that in either case "it is what is NOT stated that usually carries the semantic load."

## BOGGLING POSSIBILITIES

Do all languages feature punning of some sort? That's impossible to ascertain with any certainty. To date, linguists have cataloged some 6,809 languages around the world, many of which are disappearing with the deaths of their last speakers. But even short of extinction, many languages remain largely undocumented, and some areas are so isolated that there may well be languages that remain completely unknown to the outside world. That said, the geographic and sociolinguistic diversity of languages in which some form of punning has been noted is so extensive that it might well be present in a majority, if not virtually all, languages.

As the late anthropologist and linguist Peter Farb wrote in *Word Play: What Happens When People Talk*, "The clear fact that emerges from an examination of the languages of the world is that they universally prohibit certain kinds of utterances—and they universally agree about other kinds." All languages, he asserted, have strict rules about the use of distinct sounds, or phonemes, and the contrasts that speakers must make between them (the initial letters of *r*ate, *d*ate and *l*ate are phonemes). Similarly, there are rules that govern the relationships between phonemes and their larger cousins, morphemes, which are sound units in a word that can't be broken down further, such as the components of the word outgoing: out-go-ing. No matter what language we speak, Farb wrote, "we follow rules that govern the way morphemes combine to produce wordlike elements, and the way these elements are further structured into sentences."

Which is not to argue that all languages necessarily permit punning or facilitate it equally. But some languages—especially those with a wealth of homophones and whose speakers value verbal dexterity—lend themselves to, and even encourage, such wordplay. But is there something about punning that is intrinsic to language itself? Where does the urge to pun come from? And what role, if any, has it played in human development?

## MANY SMALL STEPS AND ONE MAMMOTH LEAP

Primitive hominids didn't pun. Evidence suggests that they couldn't even speak, at least not in any way we might recognize as speech. Physiologically, their brains, spinal structure, nerves and vocal musculature were not capable of anything but the simplest vocalizations. But about a million years ago, evolutionary changes that favored those able to do more than just grunt began to accelerate.

Steven Fischer, the author of *A History of Language*, notes that it is important to differentiate modern human speech from that of animals and insects, many of which have evolved to communicate complex information among large organizations, such as ants (which signal one another, in part, using chemicals) and bees (which do a "dance" to indicate the precise location of pollen sources that might be miles away). Fischer argues that human speech is qualitatively different from the communication of such other species because it is dynamic and self-referential, enriched and enabled by abstract words such as to, of, which, because and why—none of which directly correlate with things in the natural world. In other words, humans developed syntax.

But how and when did this happen? Patterns of hominid

migration about 900,000 years ago, documented through pale-
ontological evidence, indicate that early human ancestors
crossed significant stretches of open water on journeys that
would have required rafts of some sort. Researchers theorize
that constructing such rafts and setting off on voyages into the
unknown would have required some capacity for abstract
thinking and collaboration. This, in turn, would have required
rudimentary speech.

By half a million years ago, groups of spear-throwing hunters in what is now England were teaming up to track and am-
bush large game, providing strong evidence that abstract
thinking and basic speech, along with mastery of fire, were enabling people to colonize and survive cold, hostile environ-
ments with increasing success. But it was not until about
150,000 years ago that people reached their modern anatomical
state as *Homo sapiens,* with the physiological capacity for advanced speech. Still, scientists believe that even with that capacity, it took another 6,000 generations before people began to put
it to real use.

It was about this time, some 35,000 years ago, in the caves of
Europe and the Middle East, that the first hard evidence of human punning arises. It takes the form of an oblong stone statu-
ette depicting a woman with breasts, belly and thighs. But
rotate it 180 degrees, and the carving becomes an erect penis.
The object is a deliberate visual pun, one whose meaning depends entirely on how you view it. Cleverly, it manages to convey two ideas simultaneously: that men and women are both
opposites and inseparable. Conceptually, it's a not-so-primitive
double entendre, and indicates that some people had not only
developed the intellectual capacity to conceptualize a pun, but
actually made them in some form, too.

## BABBLE ON

Genesis recounts that, in the wake of the Great Flood, all people spoke a common language and began to prosper. But when a group of Babylonian strivers started building a soaring tower designed to touch the heavens, God became angry; the Tower of Babel was clearly not intended as a monument to Him, but rather to human ego. And so the Almighty decided to "confound their language, that they may not understand each other's speech." Then as now, dealing with contractors was hard enough; by sundering people's ability to communicate with one another, God had effectively issued a stop-work order of biblical proportions. Hubris so trumped, the project spiraled into ruin.

Genesis makes no mention of exactly who led the building effort or precisely where the tower was built. However, scholars believe that the story is likely based on an actual, massive ziggurat erected by an Assyrian king in Babylon (now an archeological site some fifty-five miles south of Baghdad) sometime before the sixth century BC. Incidentally, scholars trace the tower's biblical name, Babel, to the archaic Hebrew word *balul*, meaning "to jumble, confuse or confound." Despite this, it's only an ironic coincidence that Babel sounds like the English word *babble*, which stems from a different etymological root altogether.

Mythic towers notwithstanding, the ancient Fertile Crescent of historical fact was indeed rich in puns during ancient times. We know this because some of history's earliest written records preserved them for posterity. Among such examples at the British Museum is a fractured clay tablet, about the size of a paperback book, which was likely inscribed for King Ammisaduqa of Babylon about 1635 BC. Its tiny, neat cuneiform script re-counts the Babylonian flood myth, including the corny puns on *kibtu* and *kukku*.

In the fascinating book *Everyday Life in Babylon and As-syria*, the late French archeologist Georges Contenau argues that ancient Sumerians and their cultural descendants—the Akkadians, Babylonians and Assyrians—all took wordplay very seriously. In fact, it wasn't considered "play" at all, in the modern sense.

"We regard a stone whose shape or colouring reminds us of some other object, merely as a freak of nature, but the Babylo-nian regarded it as a sign, and a warning of a positive relationship between the two objects, reinforced if they happened to possess similar names," Contenau wrote. "The same instinct must also have been responsible for the taste for the riddles which the vari-ous princes used to ask each other, in their desire to assert their intellectual superiority, which at that date was, or was claimed to be, as highly valued as superior physical strength."

In answering riddles or divining the meaning of various signs, choosing the correct meaning of a pun was a way of as-certaining the intent of man and god alike. For the Sumerians, a cuneiform sign "was in its very nature something of a riddle, and the scribes often deliberately wrote it in the form which would tax the reader's ingenuity most severely."

This is in part due to the nature of cuneiform script itself, which is believed to be (along with contemporaneous Egyptian hieroglyphs) one of history's first written languages. It origi-nated sometime before 3000 BC as a series of commercially re-lated pictograms inscribed in clay tokens. Hypothetically, an image of a sheep would have meant just that, a sheep. Three sheep would have represented three sheep. And for purposes of simple tallies, taxation and transactions, that worked. But as the quantity and complexity of information increases, this literalist strategy reveals its limitations. While it's easy enough to represent a few objects, how about large quantities, abstractions such as time and belief, detailed land contracts or nuanced actions?

Experimenting over centuries, successive Sumerian scribes eventually combined pictograms to communicate more complex ideas, such as verbs. As Jared Diamond notes in *Guns, Germs and Steel,* they created the written verb "to eat" by uniting the signs for bread and head—a portmanteau not unlike the modern combination of breakfast and lunch that, as noted earlier, enables us to express the concept of brunch (both a noun and a verb).

The Sumerian scribes' next conceptual breakthrough—a revolutionary one—was adopting a system of phonetic representation. Instead of adhering entirely to one-to-one representation, scribes started breaking apart symbols, meanings and sounds. Using increasingly abstract and streamlined pictograms, they could now spell things phonetically, enabling them to quickly and accurately describe an enormous range of ideas in written language. Diamond describes this as "perhaps the most important single step in the whole history of writing."

For instance, Diamond notes that it is easy to draw an arrow, but hard to draw a concise pictogram meaning "life." In Sumerian, however, both were pronounced *ti*; eventually, a pictogram of an arrow carried both meanings. Its ambiguity was clarified by other, silent marks. Linguists call this phonetic substitution of a word's syllabic components the rebus principle. A modern English example would be the text message *cu 2morrow* @5, for "see you tomorrow at five."

We take this efficiency for granted now, but five thousand years ago, the idea was novel. But even with this new ability, approximating speech in writing remained a challenge. As a Sumerian scribe summed up the challenge, "A scribe whose hand matches the mouth, he is indeed a scribe." Its stylistic and grammatical shortcomings aside, cuneiform script became so efficient that it even outlasted the Sumerians who created it. For thousands of years, their successors in the region, the Akkadians, spoke a different language altogether, but adopted the Sumerian cuneiform script to record it. And when Babylonian emerged as an Akkadian dialect, it was written using cuneiform, too.

Meanwhile, about five hundred miles to the west of Sumer, Egyptians were wrestling with similar challenges, and discovering the same ideas. Most people today are roughly familiar with Egypt's famous hieroglyphs that, along with the Sphinx and the pyramids at Giza, have come to represent archetypal mysteries of the ancient world. And they were indeed mysteries for nearly two millennia, until soldiers with Napoleon Bonaparte's army, strengthening fortifications near the Egyptian town of Rashid in 1799, unearthed a large stone slab inscribed with an ancient royal decree.

Part of a larger stone column whose other pieces were missing, the flat black slab featured three sections of text, each carved in a separate script: Egyptian hieroglyphs, Egyptian Demotic script (a stylized form of hieroglyphic shorthand) and Greek. French scientists who accompanied the military expedition immediately recognized the potential importance of the discovery. Given that they knew how to read ancient Greek, could this Rosetta Stone, as it was quickly dubbed, unlock the lost meaning of the hieroglyphs? Once the 1,676-pound block was hauled to Cairo, even Napoleon himself came to take a look.

The French general's visit was short, as was his control over Egypt and the Rosetta Stone itself. By 1801, he had been ousted by the British, and by 1802, the Rosetta Stone was on proud display in London at the British Museum. It took another twenty years and a Frenchman, Jean-François Champollion, to crack the basic code, but the Rosetta Stone eventually enabled scholars to begin learning a language that had long been given up for dead. And as it turns out, ancient Egyptians were, like the Sumerians, avid punsters.

Richard Parkinson is the British Museum's Assistant Keeper, or curator, for Ancient Egypt and the Sudan. He has noted that wordplay in general, and puns specifically, were deeply interwoven into the language, life and religion of the ancient Egyptians, who put great emphasis on written and spoken eloquence.

"The idea of wordplay is there right from the beginning. The principle of punning in poetry goes back to the pyramid texts," he said. "It's fair to assume that there was fun punning in daily life, but it's just less well attested." Puns in ancient Egypt operated on three levels, according to Parkinson. On a substantive level, they played a huge role in secular poetry and religious texts. As an example, he cites a fragment recovered from around 1800 BC, in which the god Seth attempts to seduce the god Horus with a pickup line that translates as "How fair is thy backside" or, in modern parlance (not Parkinson's), "Nice ass." To those who can read the original hieroglyphs, Seth is punning on the coincidental and convenient phonetic overlap between the words for *backside* and *strength*. One might call it a cheeky double entendre.

On a second level, ancient Eygpt's Hieratic (and later, Demotic) script system—a cursive, scribal shorthand—was derived largely from abstract, stylized hieroglyphs whose forms had been decoupled from their original meanings, and employed largely for their phonetic value. The Demotic script inscribed on the Rosetta Stone is a streamlined variation of this.

The third level comprises the prolific use of specialized, figurative hieroglyphs. Some were strictly visual, used to communicate a specific action. On the Rosetta Stone, a scribe combined the pictogram for "hole" with the pictogram for "serpent" to depict a serpent leaving a hole. Comparing this with its corresponding word in ancient Greek, scholars translated it as "go forth." In other words, it wasn't intended to be a funny pun, but a practical one in a relatively cumbersome language. Such puns were not uncommon in Egypt. Centuries before the Rosetta Stone, according to scholars, wealthy Egyptians often had their tombs engraved with hieroglyphic double meanings as a way to capture the interest of literate passersby.

In the face of Roman occupation, which began in the first century BC, the use of extreme punning hieroglyphs came into fashion, according to Parkinson. One such example is a hymn that was inscribed in the hall of a temple at Esna sometime in the first century AD. Apparently an homage to Sobek, the crocodile god, it is written almost exclusively using variations of the crocodile glyph.

But Parkinson concedes, with frustration, that modern Egyptologists still don't understand most of these toothsome, grinning puns. "You can see the crocodiles, but they're so convoluted that we don't know what it means. It looks wonderful, but we just can't read the damn thing!"

## LETTER RIP

In hindsight, it's hard to understand why neither the Egyptians nor scribes of the Fertile Crescent took the next logical step: to create a true alphabet. With all the conceptual tools in place, including the ability to decouple and recouple sound, symbol and meaning, why wouldn't they have simplified their systems of writing even further by doing away with stylized pictograms altogether?

The answer isn't clear. Nor is the identity of the brilliant person, or people, who ultimately embraced this novel idea of symbol-for-sound and, sometime before 1700 BC, reduced roughly seven hundred hieroglyphs to the world's first alphabet of thirty characters, which modern scholars call North Semitic. Evidence suggests that the breakthrough might have taken place in the Sinai desert, or perhaps in what is today Israel. Immensely practical for detailed recordkeeping, it soon caught on in various forms, carried by—and at the same time facilitating—seaborne commerce throughout the eastern Mediterranean. Trading records from the period show the North Semitic alphabet in widespread use in Canaan and Phoenicia, including areas of what is today Egypt, Israel, Jordan, Lebanon and Syria.

From it emerged many diverse alphabets, each with their own modifications, including Phoenician, Hebrew, Greek, Arabic, Latin, Persian, French, Russian, English, the scripts of Ethiopia and those of the Indian subcontinent, including Sanskrit. Incidentally, the word *alphabet* is a meld pun of the first letters of the Greek sequence "alpha and beta," much as the word *brunch* (mentioned earlier) is a meld pun of "breakfast and lunch." The widespread embrace of the term *alphabet* testifies to the lasting global impact of Greek innovations in the field, specifically the addition of characters representing vowels, sometime about 1000 BC.

"At the end of this process," wrote Fischer, "the ingenious Greek scribes possessed a small, workable alphabet of letters for both individual consonants and vowels. All they had to do to write their language was to combine the consonants and vowels together in spoken sequence to form entire words, the same method we use today." It was an invention of remarkable practicality and power, and unique in human history. Yes, the Romans would later modify the Greek system, as did Charlemagne (who added *W, U* and *J*), to give us the alphabet we know today. But conceptually, these refinements were the equivalent of hitting linguistic singles, and nothing compared to the Greeks' original homer.

In the modern world, learning one's ABCs is considered elementary learning. But when the alphabet as we know it was invented, its impact was dramatic and lasting. As Diamond notes in *Guns, Germs and Steel*, writing made it possible for rulers and traders to organize expeditions, map and describe their routes, motivate others to follow and tell them what they needed to bring in order to succeed. "Writing marched together with weapons, microbes, and centralized political organization as a modern agent of conquest," he wrote.

This included the conquest of ideas. In the broadest terms, alphabetic writing suddenly endowed humans with the means to transmit detailed information with accuracy, both over distance and time. This enabled us to accumulate and expand upon human knowledge; to explore, explain and exchange increasingly complex ideas; to articulate challenging questions and search out novel answers—all critical to the sudden acceleration of human knowledge and achievement after hundreds of thousands of years of glacial progress.

What enabled this key breakthrough? Again it was the human capacity to recognize the distinctions between sound, symbol and meaning, and our inclination to recombine them in assemblages of infinite variety—in a word, punning. Yes, the alphabet and the human progress it subsequently made possible flowed directly from both our ability and inclination to make puns. This is not to suggest that punning has been the only key to human progress; far from it. But it was essentially punning—intentional and increasingly complex punning—that laid the foundation for alphabetic writing as we know it, which in turn made possible the accumulation of knowledge and the creation of the modern world.

How's that for pun-intended consequences?

CHAPTER 5

# *More Than Some Antics: Why Puns Matter*

THE GREAT PYRAMID AT GIZA WAS ALREADY TWO THOUSAND years old when, half a world away, Chinese potentates began constructing a series of long walls to keep out marauding raiders from the north. Over the next fifteen centuries, the fortifications they built and rebuilt eventually came to stretch for some 5,500 miles, and became known as the Great Wall of China. Today, apart from a few sections restored for tourists, much of the Great Wall lies in ruins. However, the siege mentality that inspired it is alive and well.

Just as ancient emperors set thousands of peasants to work

building walls of earth and stone, modern Chinese leaders have recruited tens of thousands of people to work on a new barrier designed to keep out the latest foreign invader: information. The Great Firewall of China, as it has been dubbed, includes a web of regulations, an unknown number of computer servers, networks of electronic eavesdropping systems, and an army of human censors—all designed to monitor its citizens' Internet use and stifle what officials suspect could threaten political and social "harmony."

To date, the authorities have been fairly successful in curtailing their citizens' access to uncensored information and in quickly muzzling public dissent, often by jailing champions of free speech. Even so, a billion people are hard to silence, especially when their language is so rich with puns.

Although the Chinese never developed an alphabetic script, Mandarin characters (which evolved, like Sumerian cuneiform and Egyptian hieroglyphs, from stylized pictograms) have both semantic and phonetic meanings. Without careful attention to context and the use of phonetic indicators (Mandarin's four tones of *ma*), listeners could be confounded by constant homophonic puns that are inherent to the language. In Chinese, puns are known as "double relations," and for centuries have played an important role in jokes, riddles and other wordplay.

In 1989, students angry at the government's massacre of democracy activists in Beijing's Tiananmen Square reportedly smashed small bottles in protest. The symbolic message? Chinese leader Deng Xiaoping's name sounds a lot like the words for "little bottle," *xiao pingzi*, and he had acquired that nickname for his ability to survive purge after purge and still bob to the surface. A shattered bottle sinks.

This Chinese propensity to pun in protest found more recent expression in the runaway sensation of the Grass Mud Horse. Variously depicted in a live-action YouTube hit, an animated rap video and a popular stuffed animal that closely resembles an alpaca, the Grass Mud Horse is an entirely fictional creation that raises a defiant phonetic middle finger to government censors. The subversion lies in the fact that, while the printed characters for Grass Mud Horse are benign, the spoken words sound like the Mandarin for "fuck your mother."

In the very popular YouTube hit, a children's chorus sings of the animal's virtues. At the same time, the lyrics are crude puns about a woman's anatomy, mother-son incest, and the way the Grass Mud Horses defeated invading "river crabs." Not coincidentally, "river crabs" sounds like the Mandarin word for *harmony*, which is the government's favorite justification (and common euphemism) for censorship.

Cui Weiping is a film critic and literary scholar at the Beijing Film Academy whose blunt criticism of government censorship and suppression of intellectual freedom has drawn sharp rebukes from Chinese authorities. In a 2010 blog posting, she wrote of the Grass Mud Horse: "I applaud the one who invented such a pun. Its underlining tone is: I know you do not allow me to say certain things. See, I am completely cooperative, right?" Elaborating, she wrote, "I am singing a cute children's song. I AM A GRASS MUD HORSE! Even though it is heard by the entire world, you can't say I've broken the law."

Similarly, Chinese supporters of 2010 Nobel Peace Prize recipient Liu Xiaobo sometimes pun on his name to express solidarity with the imprisoned democracy activist. In Chinese, his name sounds a lot like the phrase for "go with the flow."

Chinese dissidents aren't the first rebels to pun their way past authority. In Nazi Germany, a certain species of black humor arose called *Flüsterwitze*, or "whispered jokes." Some of these rested on clever but deniable wordplay. As the joke by Munich comedian Weiss Ferdl went, an art collector acquired portraits of Adolf Hitler, Herman Göring and Joseph Goebbels, then asked a friend the proper way to display them. "Should one hang them or put them up against the wall?" In that same spirit, Italians suffering under Mussolini made frequent puns about the *Foro Mussolini*, a Roman square renamed for the fascist dictator. In addition to "square," though, *foro* can mean "hole"—as in a certain bodily orifice.

In the years after World War II, the U.S. House of Representatives' Un-American Activities Committee began investigating a wide range of academics, progressives, artists and writers whom they suspected of communist leanings. One of them was the poet Louis Untermeyer, who was also a panelist on the TV game show *What's My Line?* until right-wing picketers forced him from the show.

Well-known for his love of puns, Untermeyer was uncowed by Congressional intimidation. And while he did harbor leftist leanings, he spared no ox. Just a few years earlier, he had written "I want to brand Trotsky's idea of teaching the young socialists how to shoot as 'a poor piece of Marxmanship. . . .'" But apparently, the dour red-baiters on Capitol Hill didn't get the joke.

At the same time, in Cold War Britain, English graffiti artists were exchanging cynical, punning commentary on what they considered to be government propaganda posted in London's Underground. In one such case, they edited a sign warning citizens to "BE ALERT!" defacing it day by day:

**"Your country needs LERTS."**

**"No, Britain has got enough LERTS now. Be
    ALOOF."**

**"No, be A LERT. There's safety in numbers."**

Recognizing the power of language to subvert authority, George Orwell added a long appendix to his novel *1984* detailing the creation of Newspeak. This was the official language under development by government authorities to "meet the ideological needs of Ingsoc, or English Socialism."

"The purpose of Newspeak was not only to provide a medium of expression for the world-view and mental habits proper to the devotees of Ingsoc, but to make all other modes of thought impossible. It was intended that when Newspeak had been adopted once and for all and Oldspeak forgotten, a heretical thought—that is, a thought diverging from the principles of Ingsoc—should be literally unthinkable, at least so far as thought is dependent on words," Orwell wrote.

"Its vocabulary was so constructed as to give exact and often very subtle expression to every meaning that a Party member could properly wish to express, while excluding all other meanings and also the possibility of arriving at them by indirect methods. This was done partly by the invention of new words, but chiefly by eliminating undesirable words and by stripping such words as remained of unorthodox meanings, and so far as possible of all secondary meanings whatever."

According to the appendix, Newspeak would be in place, and dictionaries correspondingly thinner, by 2050. At that time, having been suitably translated and sanitized, the origi-

nal works of writers such as Shakespeare, Milton and Swift
would be destroyed.

It's interesting to note that Orwell dated the likely extinction
of double meanings so far into the future, perhaps because
puns often seem to propagate in direct proportion to efforts
aimed at suppressing them. Tell someone they can't say something, and they'll find another way, much as a river will eventually find a way round any mountain on its journey to the sea.


GARY GOSSEN, THE ANTHROPOLOGIST, ARGUES THAT THE MORE
rigid a society becomes, the greater its reliance on subtexts,
especially puns, to address sensitive or taboo topics. "I think
punning is a code for talking about what is socially awkward or
difficult. They don't do it just because it's funny; they do it to
comment on highly asymmetrical relations between genders,
races and economic status," he said. "The more rigid the rules
of social class, ethnic and gender separation, the more likely it
will be that punning—and related fun, with it—will be
practiced as a way of mitigating the frustration."

Perhaps that explains the enduring popularity of puns, despite a certain stigma, in England. As the British pun scholar
Walter Redfern notes in his classic book *Puns*, snobbish elements within British society are loath to admit that punning
even exists, let alone thrives. Yet it does. From Monty Python
films to the BBC to the wacky standup comedy of Tim Vine,
the pun never sets on the British Empire.

And that tongue-in-cheek subversion is a welcome antidote to
darker possibilities: While Orwell's grim vision of total state surveillance and control has not yet come to pass, one recent study estimated that 4.8 million closed-circuit cameras are already

monitoring English streets and buildings—more cameras per capita than in any country on earth. One wonders what the conservative political philosopher Edmund Burke might have said about the creeping reach of state authority and surveillance in modern Britain. Long fearful of an unconstrained monarchy, he had once drily asked: "What is majesty, when stripped of its externals, but a jest?"

Subversive punning highlights the challenges of controlling what people say, let alone think. In a commentary on the Bhagavad Gita, the sacred Hindu scripture, Bhaktivinoda Thakura, a nineteenth-century Bengali poet, educator and philosopher penned a long Sanskrit poem entitled *Rusika-Ranjana*. Unlike English, which divides words and sentences with spaces, capitalization and punctuation, Sanskrit text flows together virtually uninterrupted, one letter connected to the next. Reading it, therefore, requires one to understand exactly how and when to parse the text.

In translation, one of the verses reads:

> One should strive at once
> to be devoted to the Absolute Self.
> Damn the man who worships Shiva only occasionally,
> only in distress.

Parsing the exact same verse slightly differently, it reads:

> One should try to get another man's wife
> to do what he wants to do.
> Damn the man who overcomes desire with pain,
> who settles for one wife,
> who conquers himself.

Given the general tenor of Thakura's work, he wasn't likely aiming for humor or even trying to promote impiety. Rather, his punning reveals the naturally competing impulses, carnal and spiritual, that lie within most people. His punning also highlights the intrinsic subjectivity of language as an expression of thought. This Sanskrit verse at once unites opposites, capturing both restraint and abandon, idealism and reality, selflessness and selfishness. In the broadest sense, Thakura's verse suggests that while controlling language may be difficult, controlling meaning is effectively impossible.

Lewis Carroll addressed the same challenge in *Through the Looking Glass*.

> "When *I* use a word," Humpty Dumpty said, in rather a scornful tone, "it means just what I choose it to mean— neither more nor less."
>
> "The question is," said Alice, "whether you *can* make words mean so many different things."

It is precisely this renegade character that gives language, and especially puns, their subversive and creative power. As Hammond and Hughes observed in *Upon the Pun*, "The puns that free language free the man."

Puns also free the mind. Consider the following from Hammond and Hughes: "There was a man in a house and he could not get out. The only furniture was a table. He rubbed his hands until they were sore. Then he sawed the table in half. Two halves made a whole. He shouted through the hole until he was hoarse, jumped on the horse and rode away." Apart from the leap from *sore* to *saw*, which is actually just a small step when pronounced in the Queen's English, the vignette flows phonetically and logically from pun to pun.

Is it nonsense? Yes, but only to a point. Ultimately, it's a demonstration of the remarkable human capacity for creative, abstract association. This is the same ability that enabled someone to see a rolling log and conceptualize a wheel (which came much later in human development than the earliest puns), to pick up a stout branch and imagine a lever, or to visualize boiling some water to create steam to drive an engine. It's about freeing our imagination to leap from one idea to the next to the next, even when those leaps seem illogical or impossible. And it is precisely that capacity to link wildly disparate ideas that enabled people, through thousands of generations of trial and error, to move from cave to skyscraper to space station, and from drum to telegraph to iPhone.

In a way, the pun was humanity's first hyperlink, a way to identify and articulate potential connections that aren't necessarily or immediately apparent. Punning was and remains a way to sling a verbal rope, in an instant, across vast conceptual canyons. It is this same urge to imagine, explore and establish new connections that fuels creativity generally, and science specifically. Not that puns are a substitute for reason, but neither is reason a substitute for imagination. If imagination didn't exist, what cause would reason have to set out on a given journey, to prove or disprove a given proposition? Puns reveal a mind free to roam frontiers of possibility, without shame or fear of being wrong.

Inevitably, not every idea or association is going to be elegant or even correct. Most aren't. But it's our very willingness to make and test hypotheses that drives progress. The importance of such a mind-set was outlined in an influential 1890 essay in *Science* magazine, entitled *The Method of Multiple Working Hypotheses*, by Thomas Chamberlin, a prominent geologist and president of the University of Wisconsin. He argued that entertaining multiple interpretations of any given set of data is not only good for science, but essential to the endeavor itself. Uncertainty, therefore, fuels curiosity and propels science forward. Similarly, ambiguity is a driving force for human progress in general.

According to the *Encyclopedia of Creativity*, "humor and creativity share similar cognitive, behavioral, and emotional processes that give the two parallel psychological implications. Creativity requires flexible examination of the connections among ideas, and humor depends on the selection and evaluation of different associations at different levels of analysis. However, an original idea that does not solve a problem is usually not considered creative. A joke that leaves the incongruity unresolved is nonsense, but might still be funny." Punning is a perfect example of such resolution—sometimes it's nonsense, sometimes not. Often, if you're open to such possibilities, it's funny.

Koestler, in *Act of Creation,* wrote that punning requires regression to "earlier, more primitive levels in the mental hierarchy, while other processes continue simultaneously on the rational surface." Tapping into these deeper, hidden mental resources while still operating one's conscious mental machinery is, Koestler argued, intrinsic to the creative process itself.

A great deal of creativity, whether in the arts, science or comedy, requires a subtle interplay between both conscious and unconscious mental processes. Often, these yield spontaneous insights—sometimes in the shower, or just after waking up—

that often seem to spring from nowhere. "The prerequisite of originality," Koestler wrote, "is the art of forgetting, at the proper moment, what we know."

Forgetting what we know can often be hard. Entirely apart from the intrinsic challenge of willfully forgetting or ignoring what we *think* we know, the insights we gain from that can also be unsettling, or destabilizing. Puns, by revealing the inherent instability of language, work in much the same way. In one sense they are a tacit acknowledgment of rules, because you have to know a rule if you're going to cleverly break it. But at the same time, by scrambling the relationship between sound, symbol and meaning, puns reveal that the words we use to define the world around us are ultimately just arbitrary signs.

In fact, nothing we say has any intrinsic meaning, except that which we assign 2 it. And if a pun's secondary meaning does not clearly echo or reinforce a conversation's greater context, such wordplay can come across as deliberate and disruptive nonsense. This is likely a principal reason why many people who strongly prefer order to ambiguity often express such antipathy, even hostility, to any and all puns.

But simply disliking puns is insufficient to make them disappear. Even Joseph Addison, who some three centuries ago managed to tarnish the pun's reputation so badly, once conceded that "The seeds of Punning are in the minds of all men, and tho' they may be subdued by Reason, Reflection, and good Sense, they will be very apt to shoot up in the greatest Genius, that is not broken and cultivated by the rules of Art."

But this famous quote, often cited in later critiques of punning, begs the question: Just exactly what "genius" has been "broken and cultivated" by art? Quite the opposite is true. A genius is necessarily someone who rejects the status quo and breaks the rules of constraint, rather than submitting to them in humble docility. It is the genius who embraces the opportunities of uncertainty by exploring new frontiers of possibility. It is the genius who, in illuminating ambiguity, drives the arts and sciences forward in the first place. Not that all who break rules are geniuses; far from it. But no genius has ever done great work after being "broken and cultivated."

Such creative masterminds have come in many forms, including brilliant playwrights, authors, scientists, philosophers, musicians and artists. And many of them were punsters, in one form or another. James Joyce wrote prose that was revolutionary in its use of punning and free association. His more accessible protégé, Samuel Beckett, shared a similar penchant for wordplay even as the world, already mired in depression, teetered on the brink of the Second World War. At one point in his 1938 novel *Murphy*, the protagonist poses the riddle: "Why did the barmaid champagne? Because the stout porter bitter." Beckett pours it on, but in a world going mad, reality itself probably seemed to be approaching the absurd.

It was with similar irreverence for the niceties of art that the noted punster Marcel Duchamp had, during the bloodbath of World War I, upended a porcelain urinal, dubbed it *Fountain*, and submitted it for display in an exhibition. Flushed with indignation, the exhibition's jurors refused to show it.

Duchamp's "ready-made" piece was in essence a visual and conceptual pun. By overturning a humble object and proclaiming it to be something similar but distinct, he forced people to question the arbitrariness of labels and the very meaning of the word *art*. Soon, artists such as Constantin Brancusi and Pablo Picasso were punning away, too. Picasso's *Bull's Head* sculpture is nothing more than bicycle handlebars (the horns) attached to a bicycle seat (the skull). Its primitivism is in some ways similar, and perhaps inspired by, some of the prehistoric paintings of bison that first appreared in natural, cavernous galleries of his native Spain some 30,000 years earlier.

Leonardo Da Vinci punned, too. In some of his paintings , he placed a tree in the background whose name was a play on that of the person in the foreground. He also doodled sequential cartoons whose images, when pronounced aloud, formed playful sentences. A generation later, the Italian Renaissance painter Giuseppe Arcimboldo canvassed the visual pun's possibilities with even broader strokes, combining fish, animals, fruits and vegetables in such a way as to create mosaic-like portraits of people.

Today visual puns still flourish, although their creators are often anonymous. The official seal of the U.S. Department of Health and Human Services features subtle line drawings of human faces that, in combination, form the image of a swooping, taloned eagle. And some European royalty still embrace punning heraldic crests; one of the graphic elements on the crest of Princess Beatrice of York is a trio of bees, for *Bee-a-trice*. Similarly, the crest of Queen Elizabeth's late mother, Elizabeth Bowes-Lyon, featured bows and lions.

Commoner examples appear in everyday text-message emoticons such as ;) and :) and :( as well as in many familiar corporate logos and brands. The letters of the FedEx logo form a subliminal arrow between the *E* and the *x*. The logo for Tostitos corn chips turns the final two *t*s into people with outstretched arms holding a chip over a bowl of salsa, which forms a red dot topping the *i*. And putting the "OW" into meow, the label of Meow Mix cat food is spelled with cat parts.

The top of Google's search page provides a steady parade of visual puns, too. Colloquially known as Google Doodles, these visual puns tweak the familiar Google logo to play off current events, historic anniversaries and popular holidays, swapping out the *O*s for visually similar symbols such as Olympic rings, Christmas wreaths or even half-eaten pierogies.

Google's name itself is a play on the word *googol*, which denotes the number $10^{100}$ (a 1 followed by 100 zeros). According to Google's Web site, the name reflects the company's mission to organize a seemingly infinite amount of information on the Web. To help achieve this, Google gives its engineers the freedom to devote 20 percent of their time to their own work-related research or projects—in other words, to let their minds wander, imagine, attempt and discover. Again, it is precisely this freedom to associate disparate ideas that fuels innovation.

"Most of the complicated systems we see in the world," writes Steven Pinker, "are *blending systems*, like geology, paint mixing, cooking, sound, light and weather. In a blending system the properties of the combination lie *between* the properties of its elements, and the properties of the elements are lost in the average or mixture." Pinker continues, "It may not be a coincidence that the two systems in the universe that most impress us with their open-ended complex design—life and mind—are based on discrete combinatorial systems."

Do creative people test associations or cook up ideas that come to nothing? Certainly, and often. Thomas Edison tried thousands of different filaments before discovering the one that illuminated his famous lightbulb. Someone later asked him if, given all the filaments that failed, he had ever gotten discouraged along the way. Edison answered no, explaining that every time a filament didn't work, he knew he'd eliminated one more wrong answer. In the end, his prototypical lightbulb not only served to illuminate darkness, but became a popular visual shorthand for any bright idea or sudden insight.

Only a few counterintuitive, even wildly speculative ideas will ultimately yield great results, but one can't know which is which before chasing them down. All progress, ultimately, is the result of playing with ideas and seeing new ways of connecting existing knowledge in such a way that the sum is greater than its constituent parts. And making such unlikely connections is the essence of punning. Without learning to pun, we might just take speech at face value and wouldn't necessarily learn to hunt for deeper, different or related meanings.

Richard Lederer, author of *Get Thee to a Punnery* and many other books on language and humor, argues that puns help us find such meaning in a chaotic world. "Human beings love uniting things that seem disparate," he said. "We love finding significance in what appears to be swirling data." A former English teacher, Lederer believes that the increasing use of digital technology actually heightens people's inclination and ability to make connections, both logically and lexically. "I think we're in a renaissance for puns," he said.

If so, that bodes well for the future. Research has suggested that the single most important predictor of intelligence, academic performance and later social success is how many words a baby hears on a regular basis, as long as those words are spoken by an engaged and present person, not broadcast over radio or TV. So if encryption theory—the idea that humor requires shared, unspoken information to "get" the joke—actually explains the evolutionary advantages of verbal humor, the most verbal among us might just end up getting in the last word for generations to come.

If such wordplay does offer an evolutionary advantage, a propensity for it might well be hardwired within us. As the late neurologist Max Levin theorized: "If play were not pleasurable, kittens would never chase each other's tails, and so would lack practice in the motor skills needed for survival. If there were no pleasure in the appreciation of the absurd, if there were no fun in playing with ideas, putting them together in various combinations and seeing what makes sense or nonsense—in brief, if there were not such a thing as humor—children would lack practice in the art of thinking, the most complex and most powerful survival tool of all."

UNDOUBTEDLY, THE MOST STUBBORN CRITICS OF THE PUN WILL probably never concede its catalytic, creative importance. Despite ample evidence to the contrary, they will insist that puns are by their very nature juvenile, foolish, or automatic groaners. But those who declaim puns categorically fail to grasp the intrinsic relationship between language, imagination, play and progress. To argue against all puns indiscriminately makes about as much sense as arguing against eating any meals while traveling, based on the fact that quality can be unpredictable.

Truly outstanding puns are indeed rare yet do their work with astounding economy, depth and even grace. Occasionally, a perfect, spontaneous pun even reveals true brilliance. The Englishman Richard Porson, a prominent eighteenth-century scholar of ancient Greek language and comedy, was relaxing at the dinner table after a long evening meal of many courses. His host asked him "Would you prefer another glass of liquor, or a candle for your bedside?" Responding in classical Greek, Por-

son said, "Neither one nor the other." His pun lay in the fact
that, phonetically, the Greek words sound almost identical to
the English phrase "neither toddy nor tallow." Even two centuries later, that pun demands a toast, and perhaps even a
nightcap.

This scholar's deft Greek wordplay brings our story of the
pun back to London's Devereux Court and the Grecian Coffee-
House, where those two earlier classicists—arguing over the
placement of an accent—once dueled to the death. Like hundreds of other coffeehouses, the Grecian eventually fell victim
to Britain's rising taste for tea and passed into history, in 1843.
But if its coffee went cold, the spirits that once gave it life are
still there, after a fashion. Today, the original building still
stands as The Devereux, a popular pub whose old beams now
echo with the boisterous debates of modern patrons, many of
them jurists from nearby courts and law firms.

Recently, on a warm Friday evening, a group of criminal
defense attorneys spilled outside onto the flagstones, beers in
hand, to celebrate the arrival of the weekend. Told of the bloody
duel that had taken place on that very spot, they seemed surprised, but only for a moment. They quickly noted that, as attorneys, they too dueled over language, its meanings and its
consequences, just as those scholars once had. It's just that the
pen was now mightier than the sword, and their thrust-and-
parry took place on paper, or in a court of law.

One pinstriped, bespectacled barrister in the group asserted
that most good courtroom lawyers are, to some extent, punsters. "Good advocates make their points not just by facts, but
by the tools of language, puns being one of them," Stephen Gilchrist said. Because at the right moment, a good pun can simultaneously make a point, amuse, and show the lawyer's

cleverness. "It's part of the joy of using language, and it's declining," Gilchrist added, suddenly a little wistful. "Kids being educated today have a far looser grip on language."

This observation would likely ring true to many of his contemporaries, and to every generation that has gone before. Language has always been in flux as words, spelling and grammar constantly mutate, along with meaning. Trying to control this evolution is like squeezing a fistful of sand—the harder you grip, the more it slips away. Over the course of human history entire civilizations, languages and alphabets have risen and fallen, even some that long seemed invincible. But through all of this epic change, over tens of thousands of years, puns and punsters have always survived. Often, it was they who actually drove such change.

Inevitably, some people will never like punning because it fogs up the lens of clarity through which they view the world and impose order, or at least the illusion of order. But if puns seem, at times, to confuse, they actually enlighten us through both laughter and insight. They keep us from taking ourselves too seriously, and sharpen our capacity for creative thinking. Ultimately, puns keep our minds alert, engaged and nimble in this quickening world, revealing new connections and fresh interpretations. And that's why, even as we hurtle into a future of uncertain opportunities, puns will always be more than some antics.

# EPILOGUE

FIFTEEN YEARS AFTER WINNING THE O. HENRY PUN-OFF WORLD Championships, I returned to Austin for the 2010 contest—not as a competitor, but as an observer. In one tough bout between an Australian and a Scotsman, the topic was horses. After several laps around the track, the Aussie said it was hard to get apples out of a tree sometimes, which is why he invented the Appaloosa. At the end of the day, though, it was a night auditor from California who out-punned the rest to claim the gilded trophy of the quarter horse.

I loved this Darwinian pun-off for its sheer entertainment

value, and all the more so because I wasn't competing. But having spent the better part of the previous year researching puns, evolution, neuroscience, wordplay and the history of language, I also had a sense that I was witnessing something greater—the echo of a story that was far older and richer than I could ever fully grasp.

When I first set out to explore the provenance and meaning of puns, I had no idea that the hunt would prove so challenging or yield such fundamental insights about language, wordplay, creativity, and the development of modern civilization. And while I had always loved making puns, I took them, ironically, at face value. Not anymore. Now I finally understand why bears go barefoot, and to me the pun will never be the same again.

# ACKNOWLEDGMENTS

GIVEN MY LIFELONG LOVE OF PUNS AND IMPROBABLE, FORTU-
itous victory at the 1995 world championships, writing *The Pun
Also Rises* might seem like an obvious and natural endeavor. But
this book was not my idea. Gillian MacKenzie, my agent, recognized its potential before I did and urged me to pursue the project. She is one of the brightest people I know and a determined
and talented punster, too. I am immeasurably grateful for her
enthusiasm, professional guidance, and friendship.

I also am very grateful to Rachel Holtzman, Megan Newman, Bill Shinker, Travers Johnson, Lisa Johnson, Beth Parker,
and the entire team at Gotham Books—from design to copy-

editing to production, sales and marketing—for recognizing the potential of the humble pun, too. From our very first meeting in the fall of 2009, they have worked hard to make this book the best it could possibly be, and I deeply appreciate their enthusiasm for the project.

I also owe a special debt of gratitude to the New York Public Library and especially to librarian Jay Barksdale. Early on in my research, I approached the reference desk in the great reading room on 42nd Street to ask a question. Jay not only answered it but also recommended an excellent book he'd just read about the history and philosophy of jokes. Even more generously, he approved my subsequent application to work in the Wertheim Study, whose tranquility and borrowing privileges enabled me to dig deeper into puns than I had ever imagined possible. Even in the age of Google, this mighty library made volumes of difference.

This book, of course, integrates the ideas of many others. I deeply appreciate the extraordinary scholarship and scientific research of hundreds of people whose work I have drawn upon, and their names appear in the bibliography. Some, however, were kind enough to share their insights or suggestions with me directly. Among them were Richard Parkinson, Noam Chomsky, Steven Pinker, Anatoly Liberman, Madhav Deshpande, Eliezer Segal, Terttu Nevalainen, Walter Redfern, Richard Lederer, Ruth Wisse, Robert Provine, Gary Gossen, Jack Rakove, Barry Dougherty, Mary Pedley, Robert Laughlin, John Haviland, and Josef Miller. Any omissions from these and the following acknowledgments are an oversight for which I humbly apologize.

In addition to these scholars, the peerless organizers and punsters of the O. Henry Pun-Off World Championships helped inspire and inform this book. The late George Mc-Clughan, now honored with an annual award in his name at the contest, was a formidable punster and a gracious opponent when we traded puns back in 1995. Emcee Gary Hallock, along with his co-emcee, Joel McColl, gave me the opportunity of a lifetime when they allowed me to enter the contest, which changed my career in ways I never could have foreseen. More recently, Gary was especially helpful as I researched the book, and he deserves high praise for making the championships a smashing success year after year.

Of course, this contest takes a team to produce, and I'm also grateful to 2010 co-emcees Brian Oakley, David Gugenheim, and Guy Ben-Moshe, as well as esteemed judges Stan Kegel, Jim Ertner, Alan Combs, Jim Gramon, David Arnsberger, and Steve Brooks, the latter a six-time champion. At the 2010 championships, the following competitors and members of the audience were kind enough to share their thoughts directly or indirectly, including Rhonda Shield, Ken Perrine, Alison Parma, Matt Otis, Ruby Collins, Larry Branch, Jacob Dodson, Mary Bashara, Bobbie Oliver, Darby Venza, Kirk Miller, Joshua Seeberg, Doug Spector, Chad Wellington, Andy Balinsky, Justin Golbabai, Kelly Dupen, Athene Persaud, Joe Sabia, Bob Dvorak, Joseph Poirier, Geoff Hambrick, Linda Eldredge, Sundance Mitchell, Kate Galbraith, Bertrand Piboin, Eirik Ott, Kai Mantsch, Gy Odom, Pete Reid, Jay Rosenberg, Jason Epstein, Tom Mitchell, Charles Wukasch, Satya Manz, Judy Dean, June Morris, Matt Pollock, and Benjamin Ziek. Thanks also go to Valerie Bennett and the team at the O. Henry Museum for their hospitality. I also appreciate Bobby Brown and Nicole Kirk for their patience as the contest ended, happy hour approached, and I kept on interviewing.

Several comedians and comedy writers offered me their professional insights into the relationship between puns and humor. These included Gilbert Gottfried, Mickey Freeman, Larry Storch, Michael Barrie, Alan Kirschenbaum, and especially Frank Santopadre, whose stories about his first job—writing jokes at the Bazooka Joe bubblegum factory in Brooklyn—were especially comical.

Others who helped make *The Pun Also Rises* the book that it is include Samara Klein, Michele Humes, Terry Edmonds, Loretta Ucelli, Sam Afridi, Lynne Eaton, Mike and Kathy McGilvray, Hugh and Liza Culverhouse, Jessica McGilvray, Sean and Carrie Gablehouse, Ken Weine, Barbara Kancelbaum, Talia Weine, Jeremy Weine, Bob Murphy, Andrew Scott, Del Blain, Patrick and Jennifer McDonough, Jock Friedly, Tamar Amalia Schoenberg, Amanda Spielman, Jordan Spielman, Martin Roz Spielman, Stanley Spielman, Victoria Spielman, Vaughn Joseph, Nourit Zimmerman, Amikam Kovner, Bonnie Slotnick, Ann Marsh, Kirk Thatcher, Laura "Pippi" Lobdell, Meaghen Brown, Erin Martin, Frank Schaefer, Jonathan Mirabito, Helen Leomar, Andrea Mirabito, Marsh Frank, Peter Van Keken, Marina Maher, Nancy Lowman Labadie, Joe Lapointe, Andrew Miller, Garth Goldstein, Mousumi Roy, Alex Toulouse-Lautrec, Naomi Starkman, Mark Weiner, Patricia Boulhosa, Richard DiLallo, Howard Sigman, Al Cain, Michael Feinstein, Jeff Marx, Geno Bicic, Jimmy You, Dan Okrent, Allan Siegal, Joseph Corn, Fiona Greenland, Mike Way, Carole Way, Barbara Fagan-Smith, Colin Smith, Mike Lynberg, Lee Callaway, Christy Lang, Sheryl Lewis, Lesli Gee, Lisa Stambaugh, Tina Rosenblum, Amy Knight, Rory McCleod, Don Evans, and Jeffrey and Hanna Coorsh. I also thank Merry Conway, whose generally contrarian perspective, extraordinary library of obscure books, and keen insights were a big help, too.

From the very inception of this book, the gang at Jack's coffee shop was exceptionally supportive and helpful as the project evolved from concept to manuscript. From the first time I mentioned the idea for this book, Brandt Goldstein (who could himself win a gold cup for punning) insisted that I write it and gave me great advice and support throughout. I am also grateful for the ideas, insights and generosity of Jack Mazzola (whose coffee fueled me up every morning), Larry Shaps, Tom Ruff, Ken Berlin, Ted Heller, Iris Johnson, Gilbert Girion, Brad Blume, Richard King, Deb Meisenzahl, Bill Meisenzahl, Dickyi Deshitsang, Marcy Heisler, Giovanna Gray, Christina Lehr, Tim Stock, Marie Stock, Sabine Stock, Hilary Sobel, Emma Barrie, Adam Saucy, Kayla Morse, Miela Siy, Marek Mroz, Saph Hall, Adam Shaljian, Akila Stewart, Noah Fuller, Chris Steigler, and especially Elisha Cooper. Elisha was a great sounding board throughout the project and even came up with the bright idea for the book's cover art, which he then painted. In a similar spirit, David Turnley, a talented photojournalist and fellow Midwesterner, was also very generous in taking my author photo.

Another great friend from the coffee shop, Richard Scott Walker, was equally enthusiastic about the project's historical dimensions, which we discussed many afternoons upon my return from the library. Sadly, Richard died shortly before I completed the final manuscript, but I think he would have really enjoyed this book. Two other late friends from Jack's were Lorraine Wilbur and Joe Colombo. Over many afternoon coffees in recent years, they too encouraged my writing and always put life into better perspective.

Just down the block from Jack's is my favorite independent bookstore: Three Lives & Company. Often, after a long day at the keyboard, I would drop by to share my progress, even if it was only a hundred words. The regular encouragement of Toby Cox, Joyce McNamara, Carol Wald, Amanda Friss, and Maura Whang kept me going. They also helped me find books I needed for research, and weighed in on the title and cover design.

Two teachers of mine played indirect but important roles in this book, too. One was my first and best English professor at Stanford, Nancy Packer, who taught me that writing is like anything else—if you practice, you get better. The other was my mentor, the late Bill Montalbano, a foreign correspondent for the *Los Angeles Times* who loved clever wordplay. One day in Madrid in 1992, when I was a scrub freelancer, we had just finished a feast of tapas near the Plaza Santa Ana and were walking back to his hotel, a beaux arts monument to luxury whose nightly tariff probably equaled a month's rent for me.

"I hope that someday, if I make it big like you, I'll be just as humble," I said.

"Don't worry," he answered, "anyone who makes such bad puns *has* to be humble."

While I have yet to make it big, I hope this book reflects some of the lessons he taught me.

Another important influence on this book was the lovely Cece Culverhouse. She joined me under the hot Texas sun for the 2010 pun championships, traipsed about chilly England as we searched for the pun's historic echoes, and always welcomed my daily updates on research and writing with great enthusiasm. Her patience, insights, suggestions, support, laughter and love made all the difference.

Finally, I thank my parents, Henry and Lana Pollack. Both are excellent writers, and their detailed input made the manuscript a lot stronger. Even more important, however, has been their unwavering love and faith in me as a son. From the time I could first speak, they taught me the beauty of language and the power of imagination. Throughout childhood, with their encouragement, my sister Sara and I traded countless knock-knock jokes. As a family, the four of us spent a lot of time punning around the dinner table and playing round after round of Boggle. Little did I know that such family wordplay would eventually lead to a lifetime of punning, a livelihood as a writer, and all the intellectual riches that only a love of language can yield. I got lucky, and hope I make them proud.

# ENDNOTES

THIS BOOK IS A WORK OF NONFICTION, THE CONTENTS OF which include original scholarship as well as material from more than two hundred books, articles, interviews, conversations, pamphlets, illustrations, songs, plays, videos, movies, TV shows, Web sites and direct observations of contemporary material and social culture. For stylistic purposes I omitted endnote numbers from the text itself. The following notes, organized by chapter and page number, identify the principal sources of key ideas, quotes and other materials I have cited in the book.

ix. Language, be it remembered, is not an abstract construction of the learned: Walt Whitman, Essay on Slang (1885), *The Cambridge Encyclopedia of the English Language*, David Crystal, Editor (Cambridge and New York: Cambridge University Press, 1995), p. 87.

CHAPTER ONE

2. Those learned pundits who would gather there: Robert Hewitt, Jr., *Coffee: Its History, Cultivation and Uses* (New York: D. Appleton and Company, 1872), p. 26.

2. Whatever the accent ought to have been: Hewitt, *Coffee*, p. 27 [italics original].

2. Carved records from the first millennium BC: Georges Contenau, *Everyday Life in Babylon and Assyria* (New York: W.W. Norton & Company, 1966), pp. 167–168.

3. In Gilgamesh, angry gods decide to flood the earth: Contenau, *Everyday Life in Babylon,* p. 194.

3. In order to calm suspicious neighbors: Contenau, *Everyday Life in Babylon*, p. 168.

3. But *ḳibtu* and *ḳukku* were also puns: Contenau, *Everyday Life in Babylon*, p. 168.

3. HOLY SHIITE read one of the paper's irreverent headlines: *New York Post*, May 17, 2005, p. A1.

4. RUMS FELLED proclaimed yet another: *New York Post*, November 9, 2006, p. A1.

4. "Keep playing!" someone shouted: *New York Daily News*, January 2, 1940, pp. 1, 23.

5. The word *mob* was clipped from *mobile vulgus*: Ernest Weekley, *The Romance of Words* (Bibliobazaar, 2008), p. 80.

5. But for all its musings: *Oxford English Dictionary*, Second Edition (Oxford: Clarendon Press, 1989), p. 832.

5. Some etymologists posit: Henry Hitchings, *The Secret Life of Words: How English Became English* (New York: Picador, 2008), p. 229.

5. Sanskrit itself means synthesized: Hitchings, *Secret Life of Words*, p. 229.

5. "Pundits," he writes: Hitchings, *Secret Life of Words*, p. 229.

6. According to Dr. Terttu Nevalainen: *The Cambridge History of the English Language*, Vol. III, 1476–1776 (New York: Cambridge University Press, 1999), p. 376.

6. The first appearance of the word *pun:* Oxford English Dictionary, Second Edition (Oxford: Clarendon Press, 1989), p. 832.

6. Other Sanskrit stowaways of the period: *Cambridge History of the English Language*, p. 376.

6. The comedy ushered in a new type: David Wiles, *Shakespeare's Clown* (Cambridge: Cambridge University Press, 2005), p. 72.

6. *Feign* means "to fake or pretend": *The Oxford Pocket Dictionary of Current English*, 2009, http://www.encyclopedia.com/doc/1O999-fain.html/.

7. And while Skeat confirms that pundit can indeed be traced: The Rev. Walter W. Skeat, Litt.D., D.C.L., LL.D, Ph.D., F.B.A. Elrington and Bosworth Professor of Anglo-Saxon in the University of Cambridge and Fellow of Christ's College, *An Etymological Dictionary of the English Language*, New Edition Revised and Enlarged, (Oxford: The Clarendon Press, 1963), pp. 484–85.

8. This stage is a mirage: The Oxford Etymologist (blog), by Anatoly Liberman, February 10, 2010, http://blog.oup.com/20110/02/pun/#more-7469/.

8. Liberman cites a 1641 production: The Oxford Etymologist (blog), February 10, 2010.

8. Liberman debunks the competing pretenders: The Oxford Etymologist (blog), February 10, 2010.

8. One sometimes wishes for a punitive expedition: The Oxford Etymologist (blog), February 10, 2010.

9. As his best educated guess at the root of *pun*, Liberman suggests: The Oxford Etymologyst (blog), February 10, 2010.

9. Carried back to England in the pockets of a sailor or two: Henry Yule and A. C. Burnell, *Hobson-Jobson: A Glossary of Colloquial Anglo-Indian Words and Phrases, and of Kindred Terms, Etymological, Historical, Geographical and Discursive* (Delhi: Munshiram Manoharlal, 1968), p. 737.

9. *Webster's* dictionary defines a pun as: *Webster's Third New International Dictionary*, Unabridged (Springfield, MA: Merriam-Webster, 1993), p. 1842.

9. But such definitions don't capture all forms: *OED*, p. 832; and *Webster's International*, p. 1842.

9. But there is a distinction between the two: Paul Hammond and Patrick Hughes, *Upon the Pun* (London: A Star Book, published by The Paperback Division of W. H. Allen & Co. Ltd., 1978), Chapter 1 (the book's pages are not numbered).

10. A play on words only works if the two things it relates are already intrinsically connected: Hammond and Hughes, *Upon the Pun*, Chapter 16.

10. By contrast, the alternate meanings of *scale* stem from the same etymological root: Hammond and Hughes, *Upon the Pun,* Chapter 1.

11. As the story goes, a long-winded congressman from the area named Felix Walker gave a lengthy and vacuous speech: Hammond and Hughes, *Upon the Pun*, Chapter 4.

11. As the polymath writer Arthur Koestler noted, the etymological roots of any given pun are irrelevant: Arthur Koestler, *The Act of Creation* (London: Hutchinson, 1964), p. 65.

11. In one particularly rigorous deconstruction of humor entitled *The Linguistic Analysis of Jokes*: Graeme Ritchie, *The Linguistic Analysis of Jokes* (London and New York: Routledge, 2004), p. 199.

12. The bride was in tears, and the cake was in tiers: Ritchie, *The Linguistic Analysis of Jokes,* p. 128.

12. "Young man," he shouted, "cunts are not for pissing in!": Hammond and Hughes, *Upon the Pun,* Chapter 20.

12. Intending to express a "half-formed wish": Hammond and Hughes, *Upon the Pun,* Chapter 20.

12. While some Spooner scholars suggest that these specific examples are likely apocryphal: William Hayter, *Spooner, A Biography* (London: W.H. Allen, A Howard & Wyndham Company, 1977), pp. 136–146; and Michael Erard, *Um . . . Slips, Stumbles and Verbal Blunders, and What They Mean* (New York: Pantheon Books, 2007), p. 16.

12. In one well-documented instance, Spooner, a minister who spoke often from the pulpit: Hayter, *Spooner,* p. 137.

12. When baptizing twins named Kate and Sydney: Rossell Hope Robbins, "The Warden's Wordplay," *Dalhousie Review* (Halifax: Review Publishing Company, Winter 1966–67), p. 463.

13. This last specimen was so ripe with possibility: Hayter, *Spooner,* p. 138.

13. According to biographer William Hayter, Spooner was embarrassed by his penchant for verbal blunders: Hayter, *Spooner,* p. 137; and Erard, *Um . . . Slips, Stumbles,* p. 16.

13. A few decades earlier, medical students in London had called them Marrowskys: *British Medical Journal,* March 14 1998; v316 (7134), p. 845; and Robbins, "The Warden's Wordplay," p. 461; and Eric Partridge, *A Dictionary of Slang and Unconventional English,* Seventh Edition (New York: MacMillan Publishing Co., Inc., 1974), p. 510.

13. According to Hayter, one reason that Spoonerisms spread so widely: Hayter, *Spooner,* p. 137.

14. Citing an 1889 article in *Scribner's,* Erard tells of a horrific train accident: Erard, *Um . . . Slips, Stumbles,* p. 26.

14. Punning away, the British humor magazine *Punch*: Hayter, *Spooner*, p. 138.

14. In *Stop Me If You've Heard This: A History and Philosophy of Jokes*, Jim Holt cites compelling evidence: Holt, *Stop Me If You've Heard This: A History and Philosophy of Jokes* (New York: W.W. Norton and Company, 2008), p. 11.

15. Holt notes that jokes were popular enough in the ancient world: Holt, *Stop Me,* p. 8.

15. A few centuries later, Marcus Tullius Cicero: Harry Thurston Peck, *Harper's Dictionary of Classical Antiquities* (New York: Harper and Brothers, 1897).

15. One rule he did practice, however, was to claim authorship: H. Bennett, "The Wit's Progress—A Study in the Life of Cicero," *The Classical Journal*, Vol. XXX, No. 4 (January 1935), p. 194.

15. The punch line is only humorous if you know: Holt, *Stop Me,* p. 13; and Graham Anderson, "ΛΗΚΥΘΙΟΝ and ΑΥΤΟΛΗ-ΚΥΘΟΣ," *The Journal of Hellenic Studies*, Vol. 101 (1981), pp. 130–132.

16. Before the Allied invasion of Normandy, derring-do members of the French Resistance: Bizarre and Risible (blog) http://haha hihiops.blogspot.com/search?q=remy/.

16. For instance, an epitaph to a nineteenth-century musician summed up his life: C. Grant Loomis, "Traditional American Word Play: Wellerisms or Yankeeisms," *American Folklore*, Vol. 8, No. 1 (January 1949), p. 1.

17. Only when he introduced the streetwise Weller did the novel take off: Florence E. Baer, "Wellerisms in The Pickwick Papers," *Folklore* (Vol. 94, No. 2, 1983), p. 173.

17. Scholars have identified the same or similar structures: Baer, "Wellerisms"; and *De Proverbio*, the Electronic Journal of International Proverb Studies (Issues 3 and 4, 1996), http://www.deproverbio.com/display.php?a=3&r=33/.

17. But original or not, and fanned by newspaper editors: Loomis, "Traditional American Word Play," pp. 1–2.

18. I definitely need another load of mulch: Adapted from Fun-With-Words.com on February 23, 2010, http://www.fun-with-words.com/tom_swifties_history.html/.

18. I absolutely love ribbons: Adapted from Fun-With-Words.com on February 23, 2010.

18. Add that to his popular Nancy Drew, Hardy Boys, Rover Boys and Bobsey Twins series: Bob Cook, *Tom Swift and His Amazing Works Catalog* (Newport Beach: Self-published, 1995), p. 3.

20. According to researchers at Indiana University's Folklore Archives: Jan Harold Brunvand, "A Classification for Shaggy Dog Stories," *The Journal of American Folklore*, Vol. 76, No. 299 (Jan–March, 1963), pp. 42–68.

20. In *The 'Shaggy Dog' Story — Its Origin, Development and Nature (with a few seemly examples)*. Eric Partridge, *The 'Shaggy Dog' Story—Its Origin, Development and Nature (with a few seemly examples)* (London: Faber and Faber Limited, 1953), p. 14.

22. In the abstract, yes. But not in the concrete!: Bennett Cerf, *Bennett Cerf's Treasury of Atrocious Puns* (New York, Evanston and London: Harper and Row, 1968), p. 42.

22. According to artificial intelligence researchers at the University of Cincinnati: Julia M. Taylor and Lawrence J. Mazlack, "Computationally Recognizing Wordplay in Jokes," *Proceedings of Cognitive Science Conference, 26th Annual Meeting of the Cognitive Science Society* (Cognitive Science Society Inc., 2004).

23. In other words, even talented programmers had trouble encoding the subtle rules: Taylor and Mazlack, "Computationally Recognizing Wordplay in Jokes."

24. The porter is suggesting that the dishonest tailor warm his seam-sealing iron: William Shakespeare, *Macbeth: The DVD Edition* (New York: Simon & Schuster, 2009), p. 62.

24. In a paper entitled "Better than the Original: Humorous Translations that Succeed": Don F. Nilsen, "Better Than the Original: Humorous Translations that Succeed," *Meta: Journal des Traducteurs/Meta: Translators' Journal*, Vol. 34, No. 1 (1989), p. 112.

24. Retranslated into English: Nilsen, "Better Than the Original."

25. It's because the Polish word: Nilsen, "Better Than the Original."

25. The horse manure: G. Legman, *No Laughing Matter: An Analysis of Sexual Humor*, Vol. I (Bloomington: Reprinted by Indiana University Press. Originally published by Grove Press as Rationale of the Dirty Joke, 1968), p. 179.

26. Well, I don't know how that American chap did it: Legman, *No Laughing Matter*, p. 179.

26. Rectitude—the formal, dignified bearing: All neologisms from *The Washington Post*.

27. Next, layer by layer, the birds were to be inserted: Alexandre Balthazar Laurent Grimod de La Reynière, *L'Almanach des Gourmands* (Paris: L'Imprimerie de Cellot, 1807), pp. 239–245.

27. Correctly anticipating that government censors would identify mandatory *redactions*: Giles MacDonogh, *A Palate in Revolution: Grimod de La Reynière and the Almanach des Gourmand* (London: Robin Clark Limited, 1987), p. 76.

28. Because the only task a real gourmand faces: Author e-mail correspondence with Michele Hume (Grimod translator), February 22, 2010.

29. Ravenous hogs had eaten his hands: MacDonogh, *A Palate in Revolution*, p. 7.

29. *Madame ma mère*, Grimod said: MacDonogh, *A Palate in Revolution*, p. 76.

29. To some eyes, however, it made him look like a hedgehog: MacDonogh, *A Palate in Revolution*, p. 20; and author email correspondence with Michele Hume (Grimod translator), February 22, 2010.

29. I'll be round tomorrow to comb your hair for you: Mac-Donogh, see preceding note.

### CHAPTER 2

31. This let him probe different parts of the brain: Hans Lüders and Youssef G. Comair, *Epilepsy Surgery* (Philadelphia: Lippincott Williams & Wilkins, Second Edition, 2001), p. 24.

32. Foerster was seeking to remove a tumor from a man's third ventricle. Koestler, *The Act of Creation,* p. 315; and *Gray's Anatomy*, 15th Edition (Reprinted by Barnes & Noble Books in 1995), p. 649; and Sandra Aamdodt and Sam Wang, *Welcome to Your Brain* (New York: Bloomsbury, 2008), p. 85.

32. Koestler described it as a gruesome kind of humor: Koestler, *The Act of Creation*, p. 316.

32. Koestler went on to note that the patient's apparently delirious punning: Koestler, *The Act of Creation*, p. 316.

32. Koestler likened such a layered, mysterious process to that of the poet: Koestler, *The Act of Creation,* pp. 316–317.

33. *Witzelsucht*, derived from the German words for "wit" and "obsession": William Alexander Newman Dorland, *Dorland's Medical Dictionary* online (Saunders, 2007).

33. Instead, it is a distinct piece of the biological makeup of our brains: Steven Pinker, *The Language Instinct* (New York: William Morrow and Company, 1994), p. 18.

33. Pinker encourages people to think of language as an instinct: Pinker, *The Language Instinct*, p. 20.

34. The system is so sensitive that it can detect: Author e-mail correspondence with Dr. Josef Miller, Adjunct Professor of Biopsychology at the University of Michigan.

34. Paleontologists believe that this adaptation helped early mammals coexist with dinosaurs: Natalie Angier, "In Mammals, a Complex Journey to the Middle Ear," *The New York Times*, October 13, 2009, p. D2.

35. Within the cochlea, however, all these tiny hairs don't just bend with the passing current: Adapted from *Gray's Anatomy*, 15th Edition (Reprinted by Barnes & Noble Books in 1995), pp. 831–850; and howstuffworks.com, http://health.howstuffworks.com/hearing5.htm/ as retrieved on March 12, 2010.

36. CHILD'S STOOL GREAT FOR USE IN GARDEN: Pinker, *The Language Instinct*, p. 79.

36. But *inside a single head*, the demands are different: Pinker, *The Language Instinct*, p. 81.

36. He suggests that people don't think in specific languages *per se*: Pinker, *The Language Instinct*, p. 81.

37. As such, Pinker says that knowing a language is knowing how to translate mentalese: Pinker, *The Language Instinct*, pp. 81–82.

37. If we had to express every concept with a different word: Author interview with Noam Chomsky, March 30, 2010.

38. It is this innate biological ability: Pinker, *The Language Instinct*, pp. 22–24 and *The Oxford Companion to the English Language*, Tom McArthur, ed. (Oxford and New York: Oxford University Press, 1992), pp. 214–215.

39. At first glance, the brain looks something like a cauliflower: Jay Jacobs, *The Eaten Word* (New York: Birch Lane Press, 1995), p. 168.

39. Immediately behind the brain stem is the cerebellum: David Crystal, *How Language Works* (Woodstock and New York: The Overlook Press, 2005), p. 171.

39. Generally speaking, the left hemisphere also dominates in organization: Crystal, *How Language Works*, pp. 173–174.

40. But within a fraction of a second, the right hemisphere springs into action: Seana Coulson and Els Severens, "Hemispheric asymmetry and pun comprehension: When cowboys have sore calves," *Brain and Language*, Volume 100 (2007), p. 172.

40. At least two other nearby structures also get to work: Crystal, *How Language Works*, pp. 176–177.

41. And in 2005, researchers from the University of California: Coulson and Severens, "Hemispheric asymmetry, and pun comprehension," p. 172.

42. An archeologist's career ended in ruins: All puns from Coulson and Severens, "Hemispheric asymmetry," pp. 185–186.

42. And while both hemispheres engage when called on to process a pun: Coulson and Severens, "Hemispheric asymmetry," p. 184.

42–43. Bayes showed how to accurately estimate the probability of various scenarios: Henry N. Pollack, *Uncertain Science, Uncertain World* (Cambridge and New York: Cambridge University Press, 2003), p. 161.

44. Only when kindness fails: John Allen Paulos, *Mathematics and Humor* (Chicago and London: A Phoenix Book, published by the University of Chicago Press, 1980), pp. 60–61.

44. The brain responds to the fit between word and context well before people have actually heard the end of the word: Jos J. A. Van Berkum, "Understanding Sentences in Context: What Brain Waves Can Tell Us," *Current Directions in Psychological Science*, Vol. 17 No. 6 (2008), p. 376.

45. The linguistic brain seems much more 'messy' and opportunistic: Van Berkum, "Understanding Sentences," p. 378.

45. According to Van Berkum, the brain actually takes shortcuts: Van Berkum, "Understanding Sentences," p. 379.

46. After priming, reaction time dropped: Cynthia G. Wible, et al., "Connectivity among semantic associates: An fMRI study of semantic priming," *Brain and Language* 97 (2006), p. 294.

46. This delay was especially pronounced among women: James H. Geer and Jeffrey S. Melton, "Sexual Content-Induced Delay With Double-Entendre Words," *Archives of Sexual Behavior*, Vol. 26, No. 3 ( 1997), p. 295.

46. If the task generates an emotion: "The Brain Breaks for Sexual Puns," *Psychology Today*, November 1, 1997, http://www.psy

chologytoday.com/articles/199711/the-brain-breaks-sexual-puns/.

46–47. Studies have found that different people actually use different combinations of brain systems: *The New York Times Book of Language and Linguistics* (Guilford, CT: The Lyons Press, 2003), pp. 60–62.

47. Afterward, they ranked those they'd classified as funny on a 1–10 scale: Eiman Azim, et al., *Proceedings of the National Academy of Sciences*, Vol. 102, No. 45 (November 8, 2005), p. 16,497.

47. This finding is consistent with evidence that women, compared to men, often have a relatively larger Broca's area: Azim, et al., *Proceedings of the National Academy of Sciences*, p. 16,500.

47. Third, the dopamine rewards they experienced when a cartoon actually did seem funny were higher: Azim, et al., *Proceedings of the National Academy of Sciences*, p. 16,500.

47–48. However, the researchers suggest that this intensity of reward might not have been due to the fact that women found a given cartoon any funnier than the men did: Azim, et al., *Proceedings of the National Academy of Sciences*, p. 16,500.

48. Laughter is literally the ritualization of rough-and-tumble play: Author interview with Robert R. Provine, April 7, 2010.

49. The ability to override so vital a function as breathing in the service of sound making was a revolutionary event: Robert R. Provine, *Laughter: A Scientific Investigation* (New York: Viking, 2000), p. 84.

49. In other words, learning to walk upright laid the physiological foundation: Provine, *Laughter: A Scientific Investigation*, pp. 86–88.

49. An efficient gait, one with less side-to-side motion, came at the cost of the wider hips: Provine, *Laughter: A Scientific Investigation*, p. 87.

49. Among those that emerged, most likely about 150,000 years ago in East Africa, were the interrelated capacities for language and

for abstract thinking: John McWhorter, *The Power of Babel* (New York: Perennial, 2003), p. 7.

49. Eventually, language and abstract thinking also enabled people to develop something else that's helpful in challenging circumstances: a sense of humor: Provine, *Laughter: A Scientific Investigation*, p. 92.

50. By broadcasting such encrypted information through a joke: Thomas Flamson and H. Clark Barrett, "The Encryption Theory of Humor: a Knowledge-Based Mechanism of Honest Signaling," *Journal of Evolutionary Psychology* 6(2008)4, pp. 261–262.

51. Modern medical studies suggest that experiencing humor may yield a wide range of health benefits: Dean Mobbs, Michael D. Greicius, et al., "Humor Modulates the Mesolimbic Reward Centers," *Neuron*, Vol. 40 (December 4, 2003), p. 1041.

51. He just had an arrow escape: *The Cambridge Encyclopedia of the English Language*, p. 408.

51. We experience humor when, under certain circumstances, the temporal-occipital junction: Mobbs, Greicius, et al., "Humor Modulates," p. 1045.

52. Alternatively, if our brain identifies the correct answer: Vinod Goel and Raymond J. Dolan, "The functional anatomy of humor: segregating cognitive and affective components," *Nature Neuroscience*, Vol. 4, No. 3 (March 2001), pp. 237–38.

52–53. We actually use different neural pathways to process puns: Goel and Dolan, "The functional anatomy of humor," pp. 237–238.

CHAPTER 3

56. A pun is *primâ facie* an insult to the person you are talking with: Oliver Wendell Holmes Sr., *The Autocrat of the Breakfast-Table* (Boston: The Riverside Press, 1858), p. 17.

56. They amuse themselves and other children: Holmes, *The Autocrat*, p. 16.

56. But if a blow were given for such cause, and death ensued: Holmes, *The Autocrat*, p. 17.

57. I think you must not understand that to use this pun would *destroy the magazine:* Daniel Menaker, *A Good Talk* (New York and Boston: Twelve, 2010), p. 172.

57. Many other prominent writers and thinkers have similarly decried them: Kenneth Muir, *The Singularity of Shakespeare and Other Essays* (Liverpool: Liverpool University Press, 1977), p. 20.

57. I would rather it should be from the paw of the lion than from the hoof of an ass: Joseph Addison, *The Spectator,* No. 61 (London, May 10, 1711).

59. It had verbs of ten types, nouns of three genders, and a complexity of endings: Bill Bryson, *The Mother Tongue: English and How It Got That Way* (Perennial, New York, 2001), pp. 50–51.

60. In official matters, both written and spoken, English was history: Bryson, *The Mother Tongue*, p. 54.

60. Meanwhile, as Normans began to intermarry with English-speakers: Bryson, *The Mother Tongue*, pp. 55–57.

61. The resulting pandemic, known as the Black Death, killed off a third of Europe's population: Joseph M. Williams, *Origins of the English Language: A Social and Linguistic History* (New York: The Free Press, 1975), p. 69.

62. Meanwhile, a renewed interest in classical literature: Williams, *Origins of the English Language*, p. 92.

62. I am of this opinion that our own tung shold be written cleane and pure: Williams, *Origins of the English Language*, p. 88.

62. Clergymen punned in the pulpit: William Mathews, LLD, *Wit and Humor: Their Use and Abuse* (Chicago: S.C. Griggs and Company, 1888), p. 234.

63. Such wordplay quickly became, according to Shakespeare scholar Hëlge Kökeritz, as much a part of sophisticated conversation as it was a stock ingredient of contemporary comedy:

Hëlge Kökeritz, *Shakespeare's Pronunciation* (New Haven: Yale University Press, 1953), pp. 54–55.

63. Shakespeare's penchant for punning, Kökeritz wrote, reflects the spirit of the age: Kökeritz, *Shakespeare's Pronunciation*, p. 55.

63. Fundamentally, though, Shakespeare and his fellow playwrights punned because puns helped engage and entertain audiences: Frankie Rubinstein, *A Dictionary of Shakespeare's Sexual Puns and Their Significance* (London: The MacMillan Press, 1989), p. x.

64. The genius of the language encouraged them: Frank P. Wilson, "Shakespeare and the Diction of Common Life," *Proceedings of the British Academy*, Vol. 27, 1941.

64. It all sounds innocent enough, but as Frankie Rubinstein notes in *A Dictionary of Shakespeare's Sexual Puns and Their Significance*, audiences of the time would have caught what were then obvious double entendres: Rubinstein, *A Dictionary of Shakespeare's Sexual Puns*, p. xi.

64. With this in mind, Kökeritz, a noted scholar of archaic English pronunciation, has suggested that perhaps as many as half of Shakespeare's homophonic puns have been lost: Kökeritz, *Shakespeare's Pronunciation*, p. 62.

64. In the second act of *Macbeth*, Lady Macbeth describes how she will incriminate the innocent: Muir, *The Singularity of Shakespeare*, p. 22.

65. According to historical accounts, the poem was put to music: Alexander M. Witherspoon and Frank J. Warnke, *Seventeenth-Century Prose and Poetry*, Second Edition (New York: Harcourt, Brace & World, Inc.), p. 759.

66. Well-constructed riddles are attractive for the same reason: Aristotle, *The Art of Rhetoric*, Book III (London: Penguin Books, 2004), p. 239.

66. Equivocal sayings are esteemed as being of the wittiest kind: Marcus Tullius Cicero, *De Oratore*, Book 2 (New York: Harper and Brothers, 1847), pp. 196, 211.

66. Conceding that puns are more usually praised for their ingenuity than for their humor: Baldesar Castiglione, *The Book of the Courtier* (New York: Penguin Books, translated 1967), p. 167.

67. Traveling entertainers, especially, were commonly viewed as vagabonds, tricksters or parasites: Anton C. Zijderveld, *Reality in a Looking-Glass* (London: Routledge & Kegan Paul, 1982), pp. 51, 149, 102.

67. In return for his loyal service, Armstrong was eventually rewarded: *Encyclopaedia Britannica*, 11th Edition, Vol. II (New York: Encyclopaedia Britannica), pp. 590–591.

68. Great praise be given to God and little *laud* to the Devil: *Encyclopaedia Britannica*, p. 590.

68. In 1637, he finally persuaded the king to oust Armstrong: *Encyclopaedia Britannica*, p. 591.

68. Laud had Prynne locked up in the Tower of London: Ethyn Williams Kirby, *William Prynne: A Study in Puritanism* (Cambridge: Harvard University Press, 1931), p. 28.

69. But when tipped on its side, the C looked just like the pope's head: Kirby, *William Prynne*, p. 39.

69. According to one account, the sentence was carried out to the very letter of the law: Kirby, *William Prynne*, pp. 43–45.

69. Half English, half Latin, it played off of the double meaning of *Stigmata Laudis*: Kirby, *William Prynne*, p. 45.

71. Instantly, Killigrew quipped that this was impossible: Puns Throughout the Ages, http://puzzles.about.com/od/wordlovers sites/a/puns_2.htm/ (other sources attribute the story, in altered form, to Samuel Johnson or suggest a French derivation).

71. Only a decade later, there were eighty-two such establishments in the city: *Eighteenth-Century Coffee-House Culture*, Vol. 1, Markman Ellis, ed. (London: Pickering & Chato, 2006), pp. xxvi–xxvii.

72. His sentence included, among other punishments, immersion in coffee: *Eighteenth-Century Coffee-House Culture*, p. 35.

72. Yes sir with all my heart, a bystander answered the chaplain: *Eighteenth-Century Coffee-House Culture*, pp. 136–137.

72. The king, taken aback by the brewing rebellion, had quickly capitulated: *Eighteenth-Century Coffee-House Culture*, pp. 95–96.

73. Lloyd's became the place for maritime news and shipping insurance: John Timbs, *Curiosities of London: Exhibiting the Rare and Remarkable Objects of Interest in the Metropolis,* A New Edition, Corrected and Enlarged (London: David Bogue, 1868), pp. 266–267.

73. You are like a waterman; you look one way, and Rowe another: Mathews, *Wit and Humor*, p. 236.

74. He often invented new words and played word games with his fellow London wits: Carole Fabricant, *Jonathan Swift: A Modest Proposal and Other Writings* (London: Penguin Books, 2009), p. xxxiv.

75. Me as a lover?: C. C. Bombaugh, *Gleanings for the Curious from the Harvest-Fields of Literature* (Philadelphia: J.B. Lippincott Company, 1874), p. 169.

75. Lie snug, and hear what critics say: Timbs, *Curiosities of London*, p. 205.

76. They aimed, he wrote, to reduce language to its simplest terms: Richard F. Jones, "Science and Language in England of the Mid-Seventeenth Century," *The Journal of English and Germanic Philology* (University of Illinois Press, July 1932), pp. 319–320.

76. More than any other linguistic defect, scientists objected to a word's possessing many meanings: Jones, "Science and Language," p. 326.

76. Physician and philosopher John Locke suggested that the study of mathematics helped free the mind: Margreta De Grazia,

"The Secularization of Language in the Seventeenth Century," in *Language and the History of Thought, Vol. XIII* (Rochester, NY: University of Rochester Press, 1995), p. 19.

76. Not only did many seventeenth-century thinkers begin to question the authority of the Hebrew alphabet: De Grazia, "The Secularization of Language," p. 25.

77. According to Alderson, this hierarchy was adjusted: Simon J. Alderson, "The Augustan Attack on the Pun," *Eighteenth-Century Life*, Vol. 20, Issue 3 (Baltimore: Johns Hopkins University Press, 1996), p. 3.

77. By 1600, in fact, about half of England's urban population could read and write: Melvyn Bragg, "The Adventure of English: The Biography of a Language" (London: Sceptre, 2003), p. 130.

77. There are only some few Footsteps of it in the Country: Alderson, "The Augustan Attack," p. 4.

78. Not too many years earlier, political opponents had publicly ridiculed his favorite coffeehouse: *Eighteenth-Century Coffee-House Culture*, p. 199.

78. In 1711, Joseph Addison and Richard Steele launched *The Spectator*: Addison, *The Spectator*, No. 10 (London, March 12, 1711).

78. The pun, he asserted, had finally been entirely banished: Addison, *The Spectator*, No. 61 (London, May 10, 1711).

78. In an anonymous 1714 satirical pamphlet: God's Revenge Against Punning, 1714 (London).

79. This does occasion the corruption of our language: God's Revenge Against Punning.

79. Despite such antipathy toward puns: God's Revenge Against Punning.

79. Rather, it was absurd, mocking and brilliant at once: For a fascinating explanation of his more obscure yet brilliant puns, see the footnotes corresponding to Swift's essay in *Jonathan Swift:*

*A Modest Proposal and Other Writings* (London: Penguin Books, 2009), pp. 329–331.

80. The antient [sic] Romans very well understood the Difference: *Jonathan Swift: A Modest Proposal*, p. 94.

80. Building his argument with pun after pun, Swift: Swift, *A Modest Proposal*, p. 94.

80. A punner must be a man of the greatest natural abilities: *ARS PUNICA, SIVE FLOS LINGUARUM. THE ART OF PUN-NING; OR, THE FLOWER OF LANGUAGES: IN SEVENTY NINE RULES; FOR THE FURTHER IMPROVEMENT OF CONVERSATION, AND HELP OF MEMORY*, as printed in *The Works of Jonathan Swift, D.D.,* Second Edition, Vol. XIII (Edinburgh: Archibald Constable and Co., 1824), pp. 390–391.

80. Included was the case of Ptolemaeus Philopunnaeus: *ARS PUN-ICA*, p. 392.

81. Pan being the god of universal nature: *ARS PUNICA,* p. 392.

81. Like punsters of all ages, the essay's author: *ARS PUNICA,* p. 409.

81. Punning is a virtue: *ARS PUNICA,* p. 409.

82. Indeed, when the coffeehouses first opened: *Tea & Coffee in the Age of Dr. Johnson*, edited by Stephanie Pickford (London: Dr. Johnson's House Trust, 2008), pp. 17–18.

83. And as a new national network of turnpikes began spreading: Paul Langford, *Eighteenth-Century Britain: A Very Short Introduction* (Oxford: Oxford University Press, 2000), p. 65.

83. Early in the eighteenth century, as one scholar has written, verbal refinement was disregarded: Dorothy Marshall, "Manners, Meals and Domestic Pastimes," in *Johnson's England,* Vol. 1 (London: Oxford University Press, 1952), p. 336.

84. True wit, or sense, never made anybody laugh: W. Ernst, *Memoirs of the Life of Philip Dormer, Fourth Earl of Chesterfield* (London: Swan Sonnenschein & Co., 1893), p. 343.

84. Given this attitude it's no surprise that Lord Chesterfield looked down on puns: The Earl of Carnarvon, *Letters of Philip Dormer, Fourth Earl of Chesterfield, to His Godson and Successor, Edited from the Originals, with a Memoir of Lord Chesterfield* (New York: MacMillan and Company, 1889), p. xlii.

84. When the punning playwright William Wycherley defended punning: Alderson, "The Augustan Attack," p. 9.

85. In an age when strict libel laws continued to proscribe a good deal of political speech: Langford, *Eighteenth-Century Britain*, pp. 20–21.

85. In 1742, when the classical scholar Elizabeth Carter drafted a proposal: Juliet Feibel, "Elizabeth Carter's Self-Pun-ishment," *Lewd and Notorious: Female Transgression in the Eighteenth Century* (Ann Arbor: University of Michigan Press 2003), p. 69.

86. Barbarous, or impure, words and expressions may be branded with some note of infamy: Samuel Johnson, *The Plan of an English Dictionary* (London: 1747), http://andromeda.rutgers.edu/~jlynch/Texts/plan.html/.

86. In recruiting financial backers: See preceding note.

87. What had taken Johnson nearly a decade to compile: Henry Hitchings, *Defining the World: The Extraordinary Story of Dr Johnson's Dictionary* (New York: Farrar, Straus and Giroux, 2005), p. 6.

87. As Johnson biographer Henry Hitchings has written, the dictionary would become an instrument of cultural imperialism: Hitchings, *Defining the World*, p. 5.

88. Today it might be hard to imagine the editor of a dictionary as a celebrity: Hitchings, *Defining the World*, p. 225.

88. He who would violate the sanctities of his Mother Tongue: Richard Lederer, *Get Thee to a Punnery* (Layton, UT: Wyrick & Company, 2006), p. 4.

89. A quibble was to him the fatal Cleopatra: *The Plays of William Shakespeare*, ed. Samuel Johnson (London, 1765), http://androm eda.rutgers.edu/~jlynch/Texts/prefabr.html/.

89. "Well," a satisfied Johnson replied: Bernard Blackmantle, *The Punster's Pocket-Book or The Art of Punning* (London: Sherwood, Gilbert, and Piper, 1826), p. 106.

90. And when the prominent Boston clergyman Mather Byles: *The Encyclopedia Americana*, Vol. 13, Frederick Converse Beach and George Edwin Rines, eds. (New York and Chicago: The Americana Company, 1904).

90. Many Native Americans, including those whom early colonists encountered, were adept punsters: Martha Champion Randle, "The Waugh Collection of Iroquois Folktales," *Proceedings of the American Philosophical Society*, Vol. 97, No. 3 (Philadelphia: The American Philosophical Society, 1953), p. 626.

90. The nicknames they gave to newcomers such as William Penn: William N. Fenton, "He-Lost-a-Bet (Howan'neyao) of the Seneca Clan," from *Strangers to Relatives: the Adoption and Naming of Anthropologists in North America* (Lincoln, NE: University of Nebraska Press, 2001), p. 81.

90. Penn was dubbed *Onas*: Henrietta Elizabeth Marshall, *This Country of Ours: The Story of the United States* (New York: George H. Doran Company, 1917), Chapter 40.

91. The most remarkeable [sic] effect of this convention as yet is the number of puns and bon mots it has generated: Thomas Jefferson, letter to Abigail Adams, Feb. 22, 1787. *The Letters of Thomas Jefferson: 1743–1826,* http://www.let.rug.nl/usa/P/tj3/writings/brf/jefl55.htm/.

91. If English had been dammed up at home: H. L. Mencken, *The American Language* (New York: Alfred A. Knopf, 1963), p. 183.

91. Davy Crockett, a legend in his own lifetime: C. Ray Hall, "Crockett vs. Boone: Who would win?" *Cincinnati Enquirer* on-

line edition, May 29, 2002 http://www.enquirer.com/editions/2002/05/29/tem_crockett_vs_boone.html/.

92. Boys, it concluded, should be prohibited from punning: Loomis, "Traditional American Word Play," p. 2.

93. Having vented, Mann proposed a truce: *Horace Mann's Letters on The Extension of Slavery into California and New Mexico and on the Duty of Congress to Provide the Trial by Jury for Alleged Fugitive Slaves*, in From Slavery to Freedom: The African-American Pamphlet Collection, 1824–1909 (Washington, D.C.: Library of Congress), p. 7.

93. There is scarcely a festive gathering: "The Philosophy of Punning," *Putnam's Monthly—A Magazine of Literature, Science, and Art*, Vol. VII (February 1856), pp. 164–165.

94. Our puns are protests against the trite and the prolix: "The Philosophy of Punning," p. 165.

94. Most likely, in an urbanizing society, corny might have been a derogative way to describe the humor of farmers: Jacobs, *The Eaten Word*, p. 54.

94. Alternatively, the British lexicographer Eric Partridge noted in his 1937 dictionary of slang: Partridge, *Dictionary of Slang*, p. 181.

95. But in the 1850s, calling something cheesy meant that it was in fashion, correct, showy, or fine: Partridge, *Dictionary of Slang*, pp. 144–145.

95. Citing the pun's classical roots and illustrious past: Mathews, *Wit and Humor*, p. 226.

95. While conceding that the professional punster who lies in wait for easy prey is a cold-blooded, hardened wretch: Mathews, *Wit and Humor*, p. 262.

95. Why it should provoke such hostility when legitimately employed, is an enigma hard to explain: Partridge, *Dictionary of Slang*, pp. 144–45.

95. Words are often not only the vehicle of thought: William Mathews, *Words: Their Use and Abuse* (Chicago: Scott, Foresman & Company, 1896), p. 82.

96. One biblical pun that Casanowicz identifies appears in Job: Immanuel Moses Casanowicz, *Paronomasia In The Old Testament* (Breinigsville, PA: Kessinger Publishing, 2009, reprint), p. 43.

97. In a similar spirit, scholars who followed Casanowicz have discovered that the Book of Job: Web site of Scott B. Noegel, Professor of Biblical and Ancient Near Eastern Studies, citing publication of "Janus Parallelism in the Book of Job," *Journal for the Study of the Old Testament Supplement,* Vol. 225 (Sheffield: Sheffield Academic Press, 1996).

97. Given the frequency and richness of biblical puns: Eliezer Segal, *History, Holidays and Halakhah* (Northvale, NJ, and Jerusalem: J. Aronson, 2000), pp. 116–117.

97. Playing off the letters of his name, they endowed him with a punning nickname: Jona Lendering, "Wars between the Jews and Romans: Simon ben Kosiba (130–136 CE)," from *LIVIUS, Articles on Ancient History,* http://www.livius.org/, pp. 2–3.

97. Ultimately, though, the Romans finally cornered and defeated Simon ben Kosiba: Lendering, "Wars between the Jews and Romans, p. 5.

98. These were humorous, often punning parodies of Talmudic scholarship: Web site of Scott B. Noegel, citing "Janus Parallelism in the Book of Job."

99. Yiddish humor is insider humor: Eric Herschthal, "Taking Humor Seriously" from *Jewish Week,* March 18, 2010, http://www.thejewishweek.com/special_sections/text_context/taking_humor_seriously/.

101. The army doctors he and his costars played: Alan Alda, "Alan Alda Discusses *M\*A\*S\*H*," Archives of American Television (Web site) http://www.youtube.com/watch?v=oIn5J6YJAmQ/.

102. Muskie roared with laughter: Lester Hyman, The Edmund S. Muskie Foundation—*Remembrances,* http://www.muskiefoun dation.org/stories.hyman.html/.

102. According to laughter researcher Robert Provine, studies have shown that laughter doesn't equal humor: Author interview with Robert R. Provine, April 7, 2010.

102. Provine argues that this common misperception has been un-duly influenced: Author interview with Robert R. Provine, April 7, 2010.

103. Puns are good, bad, and indifferent: Henry Fowler, *Modern English Usage* (Oxford and London: Oxford University Press, 1947), p. 474.

103. The rapper André 3000, of OutKast, explained his decision to get married with the following verse: Sasha Frere-Jones, "Put Your Left Foot In," *The New Yorker* (August 2, 2010), p. 75.

105. Studies also indicate that children's facility with language has a major impact on their ability to excel: David Crystal, *How Language Works*, p. 479.

105. Mississippi said to Missouri: Susan Stewart, *Nonsense: Aspects of Intertextuality in Folklore and Literature* (Baltimore: The Johns Hopkins University Press, 1979), p. 162.

106. In *Headless Body in Topless Bar*, a collection of *New York Post* headlines: The Staff of *New York Post, Headless Body in Topless Bar: The Best Headlines from America's Favorite Newspaper* (New York: HarperEntertainment, 2007), p. viii.

107. Even William Shakespeare couldn't get his puns past our copy desk: Joe Lapointe, author interview, November 17, 2009.

107. OFFICER, THAT'S NOT JAZZ, I SAY, IT'S FELONIOUS JUNK!: *The New York Times*, December 13, 2009. p. WK3

108. A 2004 study by Dutch researchers found that consumers actually preferred punning product slogans: Margot van Mulken, Renske van Enchot-van Dijk and Hans Hoeken, "Puns, Rele-

vance and Appreciation in Advertisements," *Journal of Pragmatics*, Vol. 37, Issue 5 (May 2005), pp. 715–716.

109. Sociologists at Central Michigan University who actually studied the pun-related groan: Bernard N. Meltzer and William J. Meltzer, "Responding to Verbal Ambiguity: The Case of Puns," *Studies in Symbolic Interaction*, Norman K. Denzin, Editor (Bingley, UK: Emerald Publishing Group, 2008), p. 154.

110. Comedian Gilbert Gottfried suggests that some people groan to demonstrate their superiority: Gilbert Gottfried, author interview, July 19, 2010.

110. Michael Barrie, a comedy writer who has collaborated with everyone: Michael Barrie, author interview, July 29, 2010.

110. As the retired Borscht Belt comedian and actor Mickey Freeman explains: Mickey Freeman, author interview, July 8, 2010.

110. Years earlier, Milton Berle suggested another reason: "Punning: the Candidate at Word and Ploy," *Time*, February 28, 1972, http://www.time.com/time/magazine/article/0,9171,905849-1,00.html/.

111. The pun-off is the one time of the year in which you can expect true appreciation: Gary Hallock, author interview, May 11, 2010.

112. In the days of Vaudeville, according to comedy writer, director and producer Alan Kirschenbaum: Alan Kirschenbaum, author interview, July 10, 2010.

113. Meanwhile, if one needs a haircut, a pedicure or even just soothing oatmeal bath: Marlin Bressi, "Worst Names for Hair Salons" (Web content) March 25, 2009, http://www.associatedcontent.com/article/1579207/worst_names_for_hair_salons.html?cat=69/.

114. Consider the Michigan company that, some years ago, emblazoned the doors of its portable toilets: Personality Rights Database, Carson v. Here's Johnny Portable Toilets, http://personalityrightsdatabase.com/index.php?title=Carson_v_Heres_Johnny_Portable_Toilets&oldid=1655/.

CHAPTER 4

117. According to the Kumulipo, the sacred Hawaiian Song of Creation: Martha Warren Beckwith, *The Kumulipo* (Chicago: University of Chicago Press, 1951), p. 1.

118. As the late anthropologist Martha Beckwith wrote of the Kumulipo: Beckwith, *The Kumulipo*, pp. 38–39.

118. In extreme cases, losers even paid with their lives: Martha Beckwith, *Hawaiian Mythology* (Honolulu: University of Hawaii Press, 1970), p. 455.

119. One by one, the nine doubters squared off against Kalapana: Beckwith, *Hawaiian Mythology*, pp. 458–459.

119–20. Even today, such punning is found around the globe: Joel Sherzer, *Speech Play and Verbal Art* (Austin: University of Texas Press, 2002), p. 35.

120. Oral poetry duels at traditional Palestinian weddings: Nadia G. Yaqub, *Pens, swords, and the springs of art: the oral poetry dueling of Palestinian weddings in Galilee* (Leiden and Boston: Brill, 2007), p. 259.

120. Receiving a string of eight cowries in return would be a welcome reply: David R. Olson, *The World on Paper: The Conceptual and Cognitive Implications of Writing and Reading* (Cambridge: Cambridge University Press, 1996), p. 100.

120. According to Maya legend, all people originally spoke the same language: Peter Farb, *Word Play: What Happens When People Talk* (New York: Alfred A. Knopf, 1973), p. 111.

121. According to anthropologist Gary Gossen, a young Chamulan man might challenge another to match wits: Gary H. Gossen, "Chamula Totzil Proverbs: Neither Fish Nor Fowl," from *Meaning in Mayan Languages*, Munro Edmonson, Editor (1973 Ethnolinguistic Studies), pp. 220–221.

121. Alternatively, the original target may also answer the verbal challenge: Farb, *Word Play*, p. 111.

121. Some of these *k'ehel k'op* duels can last for hundreds of exchanges: Gossen, "Chamula Totzil Proverbs," pp. 226–229.

121. Not all *k'ehel k'op* duels feature puns: Gossen, "Chamula Totzil Proverbs," p. 227.

122. To date, linguists have cataloged some 6,809 languages: Stephen R. Anderson, *How Many Languages Are There in the World?* (Washington, D.C.: Linguistic Society of America, undated), pp. 1–2, http://www.lsadc.org/info/pdf_files/howmany.pdf/.

122. As the late anthropologist and linguist Peter Farb wrote in *Word Play*: Farb, *Word Play*, p. 318.

122. No matter what language we speak, Farb wrote, we follow rules: See preceding note.

123–24. Patterns of hominid migration about 900,000 years ago: Steven Roger Fischer, *A History of Language* (London: Reaktion Books, 1999), pp. 38–39.

124. By half a million years ago, groups of spear-throwing hunters in what is now England: Fischer, *A History of Language*, p. 42.

124. But it was not until about 150,000 years ago that people reached: Fischer, *A History of Language*, p. 51.

124. It was about this time, some 35,000 years ago: Hammond and Hughes, *Upon the Pun*, Chapter 9.

125. Genesis recounts that, in the wake of the Great Flood: King James Bible, Book of Genesis, Chapter 11, Verse 7 (New York: Meridian, 1974), p. 16.

126. We regard a stone whose shape or colouring reminds us of some other object: Contenau, *Everyday Life in Babylon*, pp. 167–168.

126. In answering riddles or divining the meaning of various signs: Contenau, *Everyday Life in Babylon*, pp. 168–69.

127. The Sumerian scribes' next conceptual breakthrough: Jared Diamond, *Guns, Germs and Steel: The Fates of Human Societies* (New York: W.W. Norton & Company, 1999), p. 220.

127. For instance, Diamond notes that it is easy to draw an arrow: Contenau, *Everyday Life in Babylon*, pp 168–69.

128. As a Sumerian scribe summed up the challenge: Fischer, *A History of Language*, p. 86.

129. The idea of wordplay is there right from the beginning: Richard B. Parkinson, author interview, June 18, 2010.

129. To those who can read the original hieroglyphs: Richard B. Parkinson, *Poetry and Culture in Middle Kingdom Egypt: A Dark Side to Perfection* (London: Continuum, 2002), p. 143.

130. Comparing this with its corresponding word in ancient Greek, scholars translated it as "go forth": Richard B. Parkinson, *Cracking Codes: The Rosetta Stone and Decipherment* (London: British Museum Press, 1999), p. 80.

130. Apparently an homage to Sobek, the crocodile god: Richard B. Parkinson, e-mail message to author, May 19, 2010.

130. But Parkinson concedes, with frustration: Richard Parkinson, author interview, June 18, 2010.

131. From it emerged many diverse alphabets: *Oxford Companion*, p. 30.

132. "At the end of this process," wrote Steven Fischer: Fischer, *A History of Language*, p. 99.

132. Writing marched together with weapons: Diamond, *Guns, Germs and Steel*, p. 216.

CHAPTER 5

137. I applaud the one who invented such a pun: Voice of Patriots (blog), http://voiceofpatriots.spaces.live.com/blog/cns!BF2D4692 42B70A0D!1139.entry/.

137. In Nazi Germany, a certain species of black humor arose called *Flüsterwitze*: Egon Larson, *Wit As a Weapon* (London: Frederick Muller Limited, 1980), pp. 53–55.

139. Your country needs LERTS: *The Cambridge Encyclopedia of the English Language*, p. 408.

139. Recognizing the power of language to subvert authority, George Orwell added a long appendix to his novel *1984* explaining the creation of Newspeak: George Orwell, *1984* (New York: Plume, 1983), p. 309.

139. Its vocabulary was so constructed as to give exact and often very subtle expression to every meaning: Orwell, *1984*, p. 310.

140. I think punning is a code for talking about what is socially awkward or difficult: Gary Gossen, author interview, August 12, 2010.

140. The more rigid the rules of social class: Orwell, *1984*, p. 310.

140. While Orwell's grim vision of total state surveillance and control has not yet come to pass: Paul Lewis, "Every step you take: UK underground centre that is spy capital of the world," *The Guardian*, March 2, 2009, http://www.guardian.co.uk/uk/2009/mar/02/westminster-cctv-system-privacy/.

141. Long fearful of an unconstrained monarchy: Mathews, *Wit and Humor*, p. 238.

141. One should strive at once to be devoted to the Absolute Self: Lee Siegel, *Laughing Matters* (Chicago: University of Chicago Press, 1987), p. 382.

142. "When *I* use a word," Humpty Dumpty said: Lewis Carroll, *Through the Looking Glass*, http://www.gutenberg.org/files/12/12-h/12-h.htm/.

142. The puns that free language free the man: Hammond and Hughes, *Upon the Pun*, Chapter 16.

142. There was a man in a house and he could not get out: Hammond and Hughes, *Upon the Pun*, Chapter 16.

144. Creativity requires flexible examination of the connections among ideas: *Encyclopedia of Creativity*, Vol. 1, Mark A. Runco

and Steven R. Pritzker, Editors-in-Chief (San Diego and London: Academic Press, 1999), p. 852.

144. Arthur Koestler, in his seminal *Act of Creation,* wrote that punning requires regression: Koestler, *The Act of Creation*, pp. 316–317.

145. The prerequisite of originality, Koestler wrote, is the art of forgetting: Koestler, *The Act of Creation*, p. 190.

145. The seeds of Punning are in the minds of all men: Lederer, *Get Thee to a Punnery*, p. 5.

146. Why did the barmaid champagne? Because the stout porter bitter: Samuel Beckett, *Murphy* (New York: Grove Press, 1957), p. 139.

147. A generation later, the Italian Renaissance painter Giuseppe Arcimboldo canvassed the visual pun's possibilities: Eli Kince, *Visual Puns in Design* (New York: Watson-Guptill Publications, a division of Billboard Publications, Inc., 1982), pp. 15–17.

148. According to Google's Web site, the name reflects the company's mission: Google Web site, http://www.google.com/corporate/history.html/ as downloaded on August 9, 2010.

148. Most of the complicated systems we see in the world, writes Steven Pinker, are *blending systems*: Pinker, *The Language Instinct*, p. 85.

149. Research has suggested that the single most important predictor of intelligence: *The New York Times Book of Language*, p. 101.

150. As the late neurologist Max Levin theorized: Walter Redfern, *Puns* (New York: Basis Blackwell Inc., 1985), p. 148.

150. Responding in classical Greek, Porson said: *The New Monthly Magazine and Literary Journal*, Part I (London: Henry Colburn, 1827), p. 272.

151. Good advocates make their points not just by facts, but by the tools of language: Stephen Gilchrist, author interview, London, June 11, 2010.

# SELECT BIBLIOGRAPHY

Aamdodt, Sandra, and Sam Wang, *Welcome to Your Brain* (New York: Bloomsbury, 2008).

Addison, Joseph, *The Spectator*, No. 61 (London, May 10, 1711).

Alderson, Simon J., "The Augustan Attack on the Pun," *Eighteenth Century Life*, Vol. 20, Issue 3 (Baltimore: Johns Hopkins University Press, 1996).

Allen, Steve, *Funny People* (New York: Stein and Day, 1981).

Anderson, Stephen R., *How Many Languages Are There in the World?* (Washington: Linguistic Society of America, undated) http://www.lsadc.org/info/pdf_files/howmany.pdf/.

Anonymous, *ARS PUNICA, SIVE FLOS LINGUARUM. THE ART OF PUNNING; OR, THE FLOWER OF LANGUAGES: IN SEVENTY-NINE RULES; FOR THE FURTHER IMPROVEMENT OF CONVERSATION, AND HELP OF MEMORY*, as printed in *The Works of Jonathan Swift, D.D.*, Second Edition, Vol. XIII (Edinburgh: Archibald Constable and Co., 1824).

Anonymous, *God's Revenge Against Punning*, 1714 (London).

Anonymous, "The Philosophy of Punning," *Putnam's Monthly—A Magazine of Literature, Science, and Art*, Vol. VII (February 1856).

Aristotle, *The Art of Rhetoric*, Book III (London: Penguin Books, 2004).

Balls, Claude, *The Tiger's Revenge* (Calcutta: Fools & Arrands, Ltd., 1873).

T.B. and T.C., *The New Pun Book* (New York and New Orleans: Carey-Stafford Company, 2006).

Beach, Frederick Converse, and George Edwin Rines, editors, *The Encyclopedia Americana*, Vol. 13 (New York and Chicago: The Americana Company, 1904).

Beckwith, Martha, *Hawaiian Mythology* (Honolulu: University of Hawaii Press, 1970).

Beckwith, Martha, *The Kumulipo* (Chicago: University of Chicago Press, 1951).

Bier, Jesse, *The Rise and Fall of American Humor* (New York, Chicago and San Francisco: Holt, Rinehart and Winston, 1968).

Blackmantle, Bernard, *The Punster's Pocket-Book or The Art of Punning* (London: Sherwood, Gilbert, and Piper, 1826).

Bombaugh, C. C., *Gleanings for the Curious from the Harvest-Fields of Literature* (Philadelphia: J.B. Lippincott Company, 1874).

Bragg, Melvyn, "The Adventure of English: The Biography of a Language" (London: Sceptre, 2003).

Bryson, Bill, *The Mother Tongue: English and How It Got That Way* (Perennial, New York, 2001).

*The Cambridge History of the English Language* (New York: Cambridge University Press, 1999).

Casanowicz, Immanuel Moses, *Paronomasia in the Old Testament* (Breinigsville, PA: Kessinger Publishing, 2009).

Castiglione, Baldesar, *The Book of the Courtier* (New York: Penguin Books, translated 1967).

Cerf, Bennett, *Bennett Cerf's Treasury of Atrocious Puns* (New York, Evanston and London: Harper and Row, 1968).

Chomsky, Noam, *On Language: Language and Responsibility* and *Reflections on Language* (New York: The New Press, 1998).

Cicero, Marcus Tullius, *De Oratore*, Book 2 (New York: Harper and Brothers, 1847).

Cogswell, David, *Chomsky for Beginners* (New York: Writers and Readers Publishing, Inc., 1996).

Cohen, Sarah Blacher, editor, *Jewish Wry: Essays on Jewish Humor* (Bloomington and Indianapolis: Indiana University Press, 1987).

Comrie, Bernard, Stephen Matthews and Maria Polinsky, editors, *The Atlas of Languages* (New York: Quarto, Inc., 1996).

Contenau, Georges, *Everyday Life in Babylon and Assyria* (New York: W.W. Norton & Company, 1966).

Coulson, Seana, and Els Severens, "Hemispheric asymmetry and pun comprehension: When cowboys have sore calves," *Brain and Language*, Vol. 100 (2007).

Crosbie, John S., *Crosbie's Dictionary of Puns* (New York: Harmony Books, 1977).

Crystal, David, *How Language Works* (Woodstock, NY, and New York: The Overlook Press, 2005).

Crystal, David, editor, *The Cambridge Encyclopedia of the English Language* (Cambridge and New York: Cambridge University Press, 1995).

Crystal, David, *The Stories of English* (New York: Penguin Books, 2004).

Danian, Elin C., and Robert J. Shearer, editors, *New Theories on the Ancient Maya* (Philadelphia: The University Museum, University of Pennsylvania, 1992).

De Grazia, Margreta, "The Secularization of Language in the Seventeenth Century," in *Language and the History of Thought, Vol. XIII* (Rochester, NY: University of Rochester Press, 1995).

Diamond, Jared, *Guns, Germs and Steel: The Fates of Human Societies* (New York: W.W. Norton & Company, 1999).

Ellis, Markman, editor, *Eighteenth-Century Coffee-House Culture*, Vols. 1–4 (London: Pickering & Chato, 2006).

Empson, William, *Seven Types of Ambiguity* (London: Chatto and Windus, 1947).

*Encyclopaedia Britannica,* 11th Edition (New York: Encyclopaedia Britannica, 1911).

Erard, Michael, *Um . . . Slips, Stumbles and Verbal Blunders, and What They Mean* (New York: Pantheon Books, 2007).

Ernst, W., *Memoirs of The Life of Philip Dormer, Fourth Earl of Chesterfield* (London: Swan Sonnenschein & Co., 1893).

Fabricant, Carole, *Jonathan Swift: A Modest Proposal and Other Writings* (London: Penguin Books, 2009).

Farb, Peter, *Word Play: What Happens When People Talk* (New York: Alfred A. Knopf, 1973).

Feibel, Juliet, "Elizabeth Carter's Self-Pun-ishment," *Lewd and Notorious: Female Transgression in the Eighteenth Century* (Ann Arbor: University of Michigan Press 2003).

Fenton, William N., "He-Lost-a-Bet (Howan'neyao) of the Seneca Clan," from *Strangers to Relatives: the Adoption and Naming of Anthropologists in North America* (Lincoln, NE: University of Nebraska Press, 2001).

Fischer, Steven Roger, *A History of Language* (London: Reaktion Books, 1999).

Flamson, Thomas, and H. Clark Barrett, "The Encryption Theory of Humor: a Knowledge-Based Mechanism of Honest Signaling," *Journal of Evolutionary Psychology*, 6(2008)4.

Fowler, Henry W., *A Dictionary of Modern English Usage* (Oxford: The Clarendon Press, 1926).

Frere-Jones, Sasha, "Put Your Left Foot In," *The New Yorker* (August 2, 2010).

Freud, Sigmund, *Jokes and Their Relation to the Unconscious*, The Standard Edition (New York and London: W.W. Norton & Company, 1960).

Gaur, Albertine, *A History of Writing* (London: The British Library, 1992).

Geer, James H., and Jeffrey S. Melton, "Sexual Content-Induced Delay With Double-Entendre Words," *Archives of Sexual Behavior*, Volume 26, Number 3 (1997).

Gossen, Gary H., "Chamula Totzil Proverbs: Neither Fish Nor Fowl," from *Meaning in Mayan Languages*, Munro Edmonson, Editor (Ethnolinguistic Studies, 1973).

Grimod de La Reynière, Alexandre Balthazar Laurent, *L'Almanach des Gourmands* (Paris: L'Imprimerie de Cellot, 1807).

Hammond, Paul, and Patrick Hughes, *Upon the Pun* (London: A Star Book, published by The Paperback Division of W. H. Allen & Co. Ltd., 1978).

Hayter, William, *Spooner, A Biography* (London: W.H. Allen, A Howard & Wyndham Company, 1977).

Hedge, Gurupad K., *Pun in Sanskrit Literature—A New Approach* (Mysore: The Director Prasaranga, University of Mysore, 1982).

Hewitt, Jr., Robert, *Coffee: Its History, Cultivation and Uses* (New York: D. Appleton and Company, 1872).

Hitchings, Henry, *Defining the World: The Extraordinary Story of Dr Johnson's Dictionary* (New York: Farrar, Straus and Giroux, 2005).

Hitchings, Henry, *The Secret Life of Words: How English Became English* (New York: Picador, 2008).

Holmes Sr., Oliver Wendell, *The Autocrat of the Breakfast-Table* (Boston: The Riverside Press, 1858).

Holt, Jim, *Stop Me If You've Heard This: A History and Philosophy of Jokes* (New York: W.W. Norton and Company, 2008).

Hyman, Lester, The Edmund S. Muskie Foundation—*Remembrances* http://www.muskiefoundation.org/stories.hyman.html/.

Jacobs, Jay, *The Eaten Word: The Language of Food, The Food in Our Language* (New York: Birch Lane Press, 1995).

Jefferson, Thomas, letter to Abigail Adams, Feb. 22, 1787. *The Letters of Thomas Jefferson: 1743-1826*, http://www.let.rug.nl/usa/P/tj3/writings/brf/jefl55.htm/.

Johnson, Samuel, *The Plan of an English Dictionary* (London: 1747), http://andromeda.rutgers.edu/~jlynch/Texts/plan.html/.

Johnson, Samuel, editor, *The Plays of William Shakespeare*, (London: 1765), http://andromeda.rutgers.edu/~jlynch/Texts/prefabr.html.

Jones, Richard F., "Science and Language in England of the Mid-Seventeenth Century," *The Journal of English and Germanic Philology* (University of Illinois Press, July 1932).

Kince, Eli, *Visual Puns in Design* (New York: Watson-Guptill Publications, a division of Billboard Publications, Inc., 1982).

Kirby, Ethyn Williams, *William Prynne: A Study in Puritanism* (Cambridge: Harvard University Press, 1931).

Koestler, Arthur, *The Act of Creation* (London: Hutchinson, 1964).

Kökeritz, Hëlge, *Shakespeare's Pronunciation* (New Haven: Yale University Press, 1953).

Langford, Paul, *Eighteenth-Century Britain: A Very Short Introduction* (Oxford: Oxford University Press, 2000).

Lanham, Richard A., *A Handlist of Rhetorical Terms*, Second Edition (Berkeley, Los Angeles, London: University of California Press, 1991).

Larson, Egon, *Wit As a Weapon* (London: Frederick Muller Limited, 1980).

Lederer, Richard, *Get Thee to a Punnery* (Layton, UT: Wyrick & Company, 2006).

Legman, G., *No Laughing Matter: An Analysis of Sexual Humor*, Vol. I (Bloomington: Reprinted by Indiana University Press. Originally published by Grove Press as *Rationale of the Dirty Joke*, 1968).

Lendering, Jona, "Wars between the Jews and Romans: Simon ben Kosiba (130 136 CE)," from *LIVIUS Articles on Ancient History*, http://www.livius.org/.

Lenneberg, Eric H., *The Biological Foundations of Language* (New York, London and Sydney: John Wiley & Sons, 1967).

Lewis, Paul, "Every step you take: UK underground centre that is spy capital of the world," *The Guardian*, March 2, 2009, http://www.guardian.co.uk/uk/2009/mar/02/westminster-cctv-system-privacy/.

Liberman, Anatoly, "The Oxford Etymologist" (blog, February 10, 2010, http://blog.oup.com/20110/02/pun/#more-7469/.)

Loomis, C. Grant, "Traditional American Word Play: Wellerisms or Yankeeisms," *Western Folklore*, Vol. 8., No. 1 (January 1949).

MacDonogh, Giles, *A Palate in Revolution: Grimod de La Reynière and the Almanach des Gourmand* (London: Robin Clark Limited, 1987).

*Horace Mann's Letters on The Extension of Slavery into California and New Mexico and on the Duty of Congress to Provide the Trial by Jury for Alleged Fugitive Slaves* in From Slavery to Freedom: The African-American Pamphlet Collection 1824–1909 (Washington, D.C.: Library of Congress).

Marshall, Dorothy, "Manners, Meals and Domestic Pastimes," in *Johnson's England,* Vol. 1 (London: Oxford University Press, 1952).

Marshall, Henrietta Elizabeth, *This Country of Ours: The Story of the United States* (New York: George H. Doran Company, 1917).

Mathews, William, *Wit and Humor: Their Use and Abuse* (Chicago: S.C. Griggs and Company, 1888).

Mathews, William, *Words: Their Use and Abuse* (Chicago: Scott, Foresman & Company, 1896).

McArthur, Tom, editor, *The Oxford Companion to the English Language* (Oxford: Oxford University Press, 1992).

McWhorter, John, *Our Magnificent Bastard Tongue: The Untold History of English* (New York: Gotham Books, 2009).

McWhorter, John, *The Power of Babel* (New York: Perennial, 2003).

Meltzer, Bernard N., and William J. Meltzer, "Responding to Verbal Ambiguity: The Case of Puns," *Studies in Symbolic Interaction*, Norman K. Denzin, Editor (Bingley, UK: Emerald Publishing Group, 2008).

Menaker, Daniel, *A Good Talk* (New York and Boston: Twelve, 2010).

Mencken, H. L., *The American Language* (New York: Alfred A. Knopf, 1963).

Monnot, Michel, *Selling America: Puns, Language and Advertising* (Lanham, MD: University Press of America, 1982).

Muir, Kenneth, *The Singularity of Shakespeare and Other Essays* (Liverpool: Liverpool University Press, 1977).

*The New Monthly Magazine and Literary Journal*, Part I (London: Henry Colburn, 1827).

*The New York Times Book of Language and Linguistics* (Guilford, CT: The Lyons Press, 2003).

Noegel, Scott B., editor, *Puns and Pundits: Word Play in the Hebrew Bible and Ancient Near Eastern Literature* (Bethesda: CDL Press, 2000).

Olson, David R., *The World on Paper: The Conceptual and Cognitive Implications of Writing and Reading* (Cambridge: Cambridge University Press, 1996).

Orr, John, *Three Studies on Homonymics* (Edinburgh: Edinburgh University Press, 1962).

Orwell, George, *1984* (New York: Plume, 1983).

Ostler, Nicholas, *Empires of the Word: A Language History of the World* (New York: HarperCollins Publishers, Inc., 2005).

*Oxford English Dictionary*, Second Edition (Oxford: Clarendon Press, 1989).

*The Oxford Pocket Dictionary of Current English*, 2009, http://www.encyclopedia.com/doc/1O999-fain.html/.

Parkinson, Richard, *Cracking Codes: The Rosetta Stone and Decipherment* (London: British Museum Press, 1999).

Parkinson, Richard, *Poetry and Culture in Middle Kingdom Egypt: A Dark Side to Perfection* (London: Continuum, 2002).

Partridge, Eric, *A Dictionary of Slang and Unconventional English*, 7th Edition (New York: MacMillan Publishing Co., 1970).

Partridge, Eric, *The 'Shaggy Dog' Story—Its Origin, Development and Nature (with a few seemly examples)* (London: Faber and Faber Limited, 1953).

Paulos, John Allen, *Mathematics and Humor* (Chicago and London: A Phoenix Book, published by the University of Chicago Press, 1980).

Peck, Harry Thurston, *Harper's Dictionary of Classical Antiquities* (New York: Harper and Brothers, 1897).

Pickford, Stephanie, editor, *Tea & Coffee in the Age of Dr. Johnson* (London: Dr. Johnson's House Trust, 2008).

Pinker, Steven, *The Language Instinct* (New York: William Morrow and Company, 1994).

Pinker, Steven, *Words and Rules: The Ingredients of Language* (New York: Basic Books, 1999).

Pollack, Henry N., *Uncertain Science, Uncertain World* (Cambridge and New York: Cambridge University Press, 2003).

Provine, Robert R., *Laughter: A Scientific Investigation* (New York: Viking, 2000).

Prynne, William, *Histrio-mastix* (1632), online at http://history.wisc.edu/sommerville/367/Prynne.htm/.

Randle, Martha Champion, "The Waugh Collection of Iroquois Folktales," *Proceedings of the American Philosophical Society,* Vol. 97, No. 3 (Philadelphia: The American Philosophical Society, 1953).

Redfern, Walter, *Puns* (New York: Basis Blackwell Inc., 1985).

Ritchie, Graeme, *The Linguistic Analysis of Jokes* (London and New York: Routledge, 2004).

Robbins, Rossell Hope, "The Warden's Wordplay," *Dalhousie Review* (Halifax: Review Publishing Company, Winter 1966–67).

Rowley, Hugh, editor, *More Puniana* (London: Chatto and Windus, 1875).

Rowley, Hugh, editor, *Puniana* (London: John Camden Hotten, 1866).

Rubinstein, Frankie, *A Dictionary of Shakespeare's Sexual Puns and Their Significance* (London: The MacMillan Press, 1989).

Runco, Mark A., and Steven R. Pritzker, editors, *Encyclopedia of Creativity* (San Diego and London: Academic Press, 1999).

Segal, Eliezer, *History, Holidays and Halakhah* (Northvale, NJ, and Jerusalem: J. Aronson, 2000).

Sherzer, Joel, *Speech Play and Verbal Art* (Austin: University of Texas Press, 2002).

Siegel, Lee, *Laughing Matters* (Chicago: University of Chicago Press, 1987).

Skeat, Walter W., *An Etymological Dictionary of the English Language*, New Edition Revised and Enlarged (Oxford: The Clarendon Press, 1963).

Steinmetz, Sol, *Semantic Antics: How and Why Words Change Meaning* (New York: Random House, 2008).

Stewart, Susan, *Nonsense: Aspects of Intertextuality in Folklore and Literature* (Baltimore: The Johns Hopkins University Press, 1979).

Swift, Jonathan, *A Modest Proposal and Other Writings* (London: Penguin Books, 2009).

Timbs, John, *Curiosities of London: Exhibiting the Rare and Remarkable Objects of Interest in the Metropolis*, A New Edition, Corrected and Enlarged (London: David Bogue, 1868).

Van Berkum, Jos J. A., "Understanding Sentences in Context: What Brain Waves Can Tell Us," *Current Directions in Psychological Science*, Vol. 17, No. 6 (2008).

Van Mulken, Margot, Renske van Enchot-van Dijk and Hans Hoeken, "Puns, Relevance and Appreciation in Advertisements," *Journal of Pragmatics*, Vol. 37, Issue 5 (May 2005).

*Webster's Third New International Dictionary*, Unabridged (Springfield, MA: Merriam-Webster, 1993).

Weekley, Ernest, *The Romance of Words* (Bibliobazaar, 2008).

Wible, Cynthia G., et al., "Connectivity among semantic associates: An fMRI study of semantic priming," *Brain and Language* 97 (2006).

Wiles, David, *Shakespeare's Clown* (Cambridge: Cambridge University Press, 2005).

Williams, Joseph M., *Origins of the English Language: A Social and Linguistic History* (New York: The Free Press, 1975).

Wilson, Frank P., "Shakespeare and the Diction of Common Life," *Proceedings of the British Academy*, Vol. 27, 1941.

Witherspoon, Alexander M., and Frank J. Warnke, *Seventeenth-Century Prose and Poetry*, Second Edition (New York: Harcourt, Brace & World, Inc., 1963).

Yaqub, Nadia G., *Pens, swords, and the springs of art: the oral poetry dueling of Palestinian weddings in Galilee* (Leiden and Boston: Brill, 2007).

Yule, Henry, and A. C. Burnell, *Hobson-Jobson: A Glossary of Colloquial Anglo-Indian Words and Phrases, and of Kindred Terms, Etymological, Historical, Geographical and Discursive* (Delhi: Munshiram Manoharlal, 1968).

Zijderveld, Anton C., *Reality in a Looking-Glass* (London: Routledge & Kegan Paul, 1982).

# INDEX